What people are saying about …

PRAYING FOR YOUR ELEPHANT

"With *Praying for Your Elephant*, Adam Stadtmiller doesn't deliver a formulaic book on how to make God do what you'd like Him to do through prayer. Rather, he gives a hopeful and compelling look at what talking to God might look like if we'd have the audacity to believe He has hope for us beyond anything we can imagine. Read this book. The time invested could change everything."

Brian Hardin, founder of Daily Audio
Bible and author of *Passages*

"Many of us are reluctant to ask anybody for anything; we don't like feeling indebted. And asking Almighty God, who already knows what we need, for something seems impertinent or superfluous. But these attitudes are flawed. Adam Stadtmiller clears away such mental debris and allows us to see God's desire for us to express our longings clearly and consistently to the One who loves us most. It's part of the relationship God longs for us to have with Him, knowing and being known."

Marshall Shelley, vice president
of *Christianity Today*

PRAYING FOR YOUR ELEPHANT

PRAYING

BOLDLY APPROACHING JESUS WITH

FOR YOUR

RADICAL AND AUDACIOUS PRAYER

ELEPHANT

ADAM STADTMILLER

David C Cook®

transforming lives together

PRAYING FOR YOUR ELEPHANT
Published by David C Cook
4050 Lee Vance View
Colorado Springs, CO 80918 U.S.A.

David C Cook Distribution Canada
55 Woodslee Avenue, Paris, Ontario, Canada N3L 3E5

David C Cook U.K., Kingsway Communications
Eastbourne, East Sussex BN23 6NT, England

The graphic circle C logo is a registered trademark of David C Cook.

The website addresses recommended throughout this book are offered as a
resource to you. These websites are not intended in any way to be or imply an
endorsement on the part of David C Cook, nor do we vouch for their content.

Bible credits appear at the back of this book.

LCCN 2014942036
ISBN 978-0-7814-1145-5
eISBN 978-0-7814-1238-4

© 2014 Adam Stadtmiller

The Team: Alex Field, Barbara Scott, Amy Konyndyk, Nick
Lee, Jack Campbell, Helen Macdonald, Karen Athen
Cover Design: Amy Konyndyk
Cover Photo: iStockphoto

Printed in the United States of America
First Edition 2014

1 2 3 4 5 6 7 8 9 10

080114

This book is dedicated to my mother, Virginia Stadtmiller, who stood in the gap at the gates of hell as I tried to throw my life away to addiction. She is the woman who taught me how to pray and whose life's motto "Prayer is always the answer!" has stood as a clarion call in my life.

CONTENTS

Acknowledgments. 11
Introduction 13

Forty Days to Praying for Your Elephants 15

SECTION I
PRAYING FOR ELEPHANTS

1. Praying for Your Elephant. 21
2. I Dare You 39
3. Identifying Your Elephants 57

SECTION II
HOW TO CAPTURE AN ELEPHANT

4. Lost in Space. 71
5. Digging for Gold 83

SECTION III
UNDERSTANDING ELEPHANTS

6. Oompa-Loompas 105
7. You Can Do Nothing 125
8. Extra-Virgin 135
9. Be the Answer 151

SECTION IV
WHEN ELEPHANTS CHARGE

10. Elephant Worship 167
11. The Elephant Graveyard 185

CONCLUSION
THE QUEST

12. Land Grab 205

Notes 219
Bible Credits 223
Small-Group Discussion Guide 225

ACKNOWLEDGMENTS

I want to give a special thanks and acknowledgment to all the members of the Praying for Your Elephant social media herd! Watching you love one another through prayer and action has been incredibly encouraging and inspiring.

INTRODUCTION

I wrote *Praying for Your Elephant* for a number of reasons, but perhaps the most important to me personally was to help free people from the refuse of shame and guilt that can so often mire their prayer lives, removing the joy that is inherent to a prayer-filled life.

While it is very possible that you have never experienced this, I would say that the majority of believers I meet have great guilt and shame when it comes to the way in which they pray. They feel they don't pray enough, don't want to ask God for too much, don't know what to pray for, and lack the faith to really see their prayers make a difference.

The effects of guilt and shame in our prayer lives are cataclysmic. Every time we allow these sinister emotions and thoughts to sully our prayers, we run the risk of binding eternity in the now and missing out on all that God has for us. This is not to say these things are not still happening in and around us; God will still have His way. It's just that we miss out on the adventure of collaborating with God when we fail to speak to Him.

One of the passions that led me to write this book is to help readers like yourself extricate all guilt from your prayers. Guilt belongs in hell with the Devil, not in your prayer life. Not having a handle on guilt will turn your times of conversational intimacy with God into a dry place. I pray that as you read *Praying for Your Elephant*, you will be encouraged to meet Jesus boldly in asking prayer.

Finally, I want to assert that this book is limited in its intentions. This is a book about asking prayer. Since prayer is an eternal commodity, there is an eternity of things to say about it. Thus, this work does not expound on the many other forms of prayer, such as silent, thanksgiving, and healing.

FORTY DAYS TO PRAYING FOR YOUR ELEPHANTS

Praying for your elephants is not a perfect science. Rather it is an exercise in creating a strategic and specific prayer list. Below are some ideas on how to do just that. The key is that for forty days you do your best to pray over and develop your prayer list. This should be a work in progress. The chart on pages 17 and 18 is provided as an example. Create your own on a separate sheet of paper or in your prayer journal. Remember, you are not aiming for perfection but rather joining God on a forty-day adventure of prayer.

    1. Create a list of ten prayer categories. For example: family, work, school, ministry, friends, finance, or even a category for fun bucket-list prayers.

2. Pray over each of your categories daily. Each
day try to add more specific requests under each
category. For instance, paying off your debt within
three years could go under the finance category.
The goal is to have ten individual prayer requests
under each of the ten category headings by the end
of this forty-day exercise. That would be a total of
one hundred prayers.

3. Make sure to note the date each time you add a
request to your list.

4. After a prayer request has been on your list for
a few days, spend some time with God imagining
deeper into that request. Rewrite the request with
any new insights you might have discovered.

5. As you pray over your prayer items each day,
continue to add more specific and strategic
elements to the request. Err on the side of
specificity rather than being vague.

6. As much as possible, try to record the date
when prayers are answered. You will be encouraged
by how God answers your prayers during these
forty days.

FAMILY	WORK	FRIENDS	THE WORLD	ELEPHANTS
1	11	21	31	41
2	12	22	32	42
3	13	23	33	43
4	14	24	34	44
5	15	25	35	45
6	16	26	36	46
7	17	27	37	47
8	18	28	38	48
9	19	29	39	49
10	20	30	40	50

#6	#7	#8	#9	#10
51	61	71	81	91
52	62	72	82	92
53	63	73	83	93
54	64	74	84	94
55	65	75	85	95
56	66	76	86	96
57	67	77	87	97
58	68	78	88	98
59	69	79	89	99
60	70	80	90	100

PRAYING FOR ELEPHANTS

In September 2013, my wife, Dawn, was introduced to the concept of praying for your elephant. She created a list of important things she wanted to pray for in her life. As time went on, of course, her list grew and morphed. She was very diligent, as was I. We went through some very difficult times all the while keeping faith that God would hear our prayers. We never gave up, we never lost faith, but it seemed like an eternity at times. We even prayed and thanked God for our difficulties, but more for the result of those trying times, which were drawing us nearer to Him. Without getting into great detail, last week was a turning point in our lives and our future. Shortly thereafter, one night in her sleep, Dawn heard the Lord whisper to her, "Do you not remember what you prayed for? Go find your list and look at it." The next morning on my way out the door to work, she stopped me cold and had to share this with me. She pulled out her original list that had maybe ten prayers on it. I was not privy to this list originally as it was hers. As I read the list I was blown away at the fact that every single prayer on that list was answered last week. God truly hears and answers prayer in His own time. Be diligent and faithful, my friends. I have chills writing this! Praise God.

—Joe's post on the Praying for Your Elephant Facebook group page

CHAPTER 1

PRAYING FOR YOUR ELEPHANT

Whatever you ask in my name, this I will do, that the Father may be glorified in the Son. If you ask me anything in my name, I will do it.
—John 14:13–14 ESV

Satan does not care how many people read about prayer if only he can keep them from praying.
—Paul E. Billheimer

PRAYING FOR ELEPHANTS WITH BIG AL

It was 5:27 a.m. when I pulled my truck into the parking lot. I had recently been hired as the youth pastor for a church in Newport Beach, California, and somehow been coerced by Big Al into agreeing to a month of 5:30 a.m. prayer.

Big Al was an adult volunteer holdover from the former regime and something of a religious hybrid, falling somewhere between an old-school Pentecostal and a modern-day charismatic.

The idea of thirty days of predawn prayer sounded like a great idea at lunch the previous Thursday, but now was a different story. Like most things related to prayer in my life, the romantic idea often supersedes the reality of actually doing it.

To make matters worse, Big Al was late. When he did arrive, he reeked of garlic. Apparently, Al had been told that eating cloves of raw garlic would relieve a wicked toothache. He had been munching on the garlic for the past two days while believing in faith that God would heal him.

As the caffeine in my cup started to work its magic, we began to pray. I pray a lot better when I'm drinking coffee. At least I think I do.

I'm not really sure of what we prayed about. I wasn't in the habit of keeping track of my prayers back then. Instead, prayer was more like an old Gatling gun, randomly spraying its requests like bullets into eternity.

When we finished praying that first day, it didn't feel like much had changed. There were no theophanies, no audible voices, no trips to the third heaven, just me, Big Al, and his garlic.

As I got up to leave, Big Al yelled, "Wait! Wait! We forgot to pray for the elephant." He was right.

In order for that phrase to make sense, I need to go back to the previous Thursday's lunch—the lunch when we found out about the elephant.

Though I had not officially started working at the church, I was aware of the importance of stability when taking over a new ministry. Keeping as much of the previous team in place was crucial, at least for the first few months. Because of this, I had planned a series of lunches to meet the former volunteers and encourage them to stay on until the group had found its ballast.

Before meeting Al for burritos that Thursday, I stopped by the new office and checked my mailbox. Back in the Internet's pre-historic days, it was common to receive hard copy catalogs in the mail advertising different and exciting things you could rent for your youth group. While the groups I led could never afford all these luxuries, they were still fun to look at. I was happy to see one such catalog sitting in my new box before leaving to meet Al. It would give us something to talk about if the conversation lagged.

Al and I hit it off right away. Al is a great man of God, crazy in a good way, but a great man of God. I love Big Al and suggest that if you don't have any quasi-Pentecostal-charismatic friends that you go find some. They are great people to know in a faith crisis or a spiritual pinch when you need the encouragement to believe.

While eating our lunch that day, we pored over the catalog, which advertised renting or buying traditional bounce houses, sumo suits, and even a Velcro wall that kids could be stuck to by catapulting them from a mini-trebuchet. All of it was amazing. All of it was expensive.

As we turned to the final page of the catalog, our jaws dropped. There it was in all its glory—the elephant. We were in awe.

Apparently, for the petty fee of $2,500, you could hire a live pachyderm to visit your youth group. Both Al and I immediately knew that we had to have it. Granted, we had no money in our coffers, but we served a big God who owned the elephants on a thousand hills, and the plans we had for those teens were worthy of nothing less. Yes, the elephant would be ours.

THE PROBLEM WITH PRAYING FOR ELEPHANTS

Praying for elephants has always created a tension in me. Surely with all the starving children in the world there is no place for opulent prayers about elephants showing up at youth groups in one of the wealthiest cities in the world. What's the point? Yet at the same time, I have this sneaking suspicion that tells me we serve a lavish God who is big enough to manage the greatest cares of this earth while still maintaining enough margin to be concerned about even the most idiosyncratic corners of our personal lives. Perhaps praying for both elephants and the plight of orphans around the world need not be mutually exclusive.

Your individual view on the spacious or confined margins of prayer will largely dictate how and what you pray for as well as your prayers' effectiveness. **The boundaries of our personal prayer lives often have less to do with biblical restrictions and more to do with the limitations we place on them.** Limitations such as guilt, or perhaps dwelling on the kinds of prayers we feel God is interested in answering, often shackle our prayers or cause us to abandon praying altogether. Like surveyors marking off a fresh parcel of sod, we tend to lay the boundary lines of our prayers far shy of their intended purposes.

This book's intention is to help you expand those boundary lines of prayer and encourage you to pray like you never have before.

SURVEYING YOUR PRAYER LIFE

While most believers pray, few in my experience spend time trying to increase the territory of their prayer lives. The time they do spend is often focused on their failures and limitations rather than reimagining their possibilities through a detailed survey of what currently exists in their discipline and adventure of prayer.

When I speak about surveying your prayer life, I mean critically thinking through not only what you believe about prayer but how you actually pray. How expansive is your view of the power of prayer? Where have you cordoned off the length and breadth of your prayers for one reason or another? Has doubt taken over where faith once stood? Would you pray for an elephant? Parking spots? Do you intercede for friends with cancer? Do you believe that a single prayer you pray on a Tuesday morning while driving to work could bring rain to a parched and drought-stricken land somewhere in the middle of Africa? Do you have faith that prayer can heal your broken marriage? What about your broken heart? Do you believe prayer is always the answer? Has prayer become your eternal fascination?

Better yet, take a moment to reimagine your prayer life in a progressive fashion. What would it look like if you pulled up the boundaries of your prayer life and set them aside? What if your prayer life had no bounds? What if it was limitless? Eternal? What if you let God be the judge of what He will accomplish through your prayers rather than allowing the limitations of your mind and flesh to shepherd your prayers? **What if your responsibility was simply prayer creation and you left God to the editorial and distribution responsibilities?**

THE DEVIL'S STUDIO APARTMENT

Samuel Chadwick once wrote that "the one concern of the devil is to keep the saints [Christians] from praying. He fears nothing from prayerless studies, prayerless work, prayerless religion. He laughs at our toil, he mocks at our wisdom, but he trembles when we pray."[1]

The less we pray, the smaller our lives will be. One of the Devil's primary tactics is to help you contain your prayer life. He has no problem with you living in a 150-square-foot luxury prayer apartment as long as you never discover that you have inherited a million-acre ranch of prayer in Montana.

Notice I said "help you contain your prayer life." This is because the Devil has no ability to contain prayer. Prayer is spiritually nuclear in nature; it is the raw material of God and His people. Prayer is out of Satan's influence. He has no power to warp or influence a prayer's trajectory to God's throne after it has been prayed. Once a prayer is unleashed, it bounces around eternity in perpetuity, burning before the throne of God like incense. In the fifth chapter of Revelation, John said, "And when he had taken it, the four living creatures and the twenty-four elders fell down before the Lamb. Each one had a harp and they were holding golden bowls full of incense, which are the prayers of God's people" (Rev. 5:8).

In speaking of the eternity of prayer, E. M. Bounds said, "He rules the Church by prayer. This lesson needs to be emphasized, iterated, and reiterated in the ears of men of modern times and brought to bear with cumulative force on the consciences of this generation whose eyes have no vision for the eternal things, whose ears are deaf toward God."[2]

This is why prayer is so spiritually dangerous for Satan. It supersedes the limitations of a mortal world. Prayer is immortal. It has no boundaries and no marker lines. Prayer holds ultimate potential. The best the Devil can hope for is that you don't pray. And much of his strategy is to discourage you from praying at all, as a prayer never prayed has zero chance of ever being answered.

THE REASON WE ASK, SEEK, AND KNOCK

Before we go any further, I need to clarify something about asking prayer and its purpose. God answers prayer, but asking prayer is not primarily about answers. Asking prayer, like all other forms of prayer, is about relationship. If you make asking prayer about answers, you're moving into dangerous spiritual territory.

When prayer is primarily about answers, our relationship with God becomes results focused. It is a soft gospel that makes our wants and desires the central focus of prayer's message. The problem is, when God is doing what we want and expect of Him, we tend to judge our spiritual worth on those results. When God says no or works outside of our time schedule, we desperately question why and are tempted to feel inadequate or unloved by God. Be assured that as you grow in the area of asking prayer, the Devil will seek to shift the focus of your prayers from relationship to results.

Christ was well aware of the relational purpose of asking prayer. In the seventh chapter of Matthew when Jesus dared His followers to ask for things like elephants in prayer, He immediately transferred the focus from the asking to the fatherly or paternal relationship that surrounds each request we make. Notice how Jesus framed asking prayer in the context of sonship:

> Ask and it will be given to you; seek and you will find; knock and the door will be opened to you. For everyone who asks receives; the one who seeks finds; and to the one who knocks, the door will be opened.
>
> Which of you, if your *son* asks for bread, will give him a stone? Or if he asks for a fish, will give him a snake? (Matt 7:7–10)

Jesus was saying that whenever you ask in prayer you open up the familial lines of communication and put yourself in a position to experience relationship with a loving and compassionate Father. In this way, asking prayer acts as a gateway to knowing God as Father. The more you ask of God, the more you will come to know Him as your Abba.

Don't get me wrong, God is also in the business of answering prayer, but the simple takeaway is that God wants you to radically ask in prayer so that you might know Him better. Each time you ask, God gets to the work of not only manifesting His kingdom on earth through your prayers but, more importantly, deepening His relationship with you through the ebb and flow of responding to those requests.

When God answers your prayers in dramatic fashion, you will grow in the knowledge of His power and care for you. When God works on His schedule instead of yours, you will come to know more about His sustaining power. And when God says no and your dreams die or perhaps you lose someone close to you, you will come to know the God of all comfort who weeps with you. (See 2 Cor. 1:3–5.) If you want to know God as Father, begin to assault the throne of heaven in asking prayer.

But this is just the beginning. As we will see in chapter 6, asking prayer promises even more and offers a dynamic threefold purpose and mission. Asking prayer not only creates deep relationship with the Father, exposing you to His love, but it is also a primary tool God uses to propagate His glory throughout the earth, increase the fruitfulness of your life, and prove to the world that you are His disciple. As you will come to see as we go forward, asking prayer is not about just getting the things we want from God.

PRAYING ONE HUNDRED PRAYERS

In order to experience all that asking prayer has to offer us, I recently challenged my congregation to begin seeking God in asking prayer. The assignment was to create a list of one hundred specific requests. The sky was the limit. The only rule was that they were not allowed to disqualify a prayer from the list based on their perception of what God might think of the prayer or because of guilt for perhaps asking for too much.

What happened next is one of the reasons I am writing this book, as I tend to follow the fruit when it comes to determining my next steps. As we began to pray in community, our prayers not only produced fruit, they yielded an orchard. Immediately, I became inundated with stories of what happened when people asked God for anything and everything in prayer.

Dan texted me, "Prayer #26 answered one week after writing it down: Rest and connection time for my wife and I. God answered things above and beyond."

Then there was Cindy who stopped me in the church courtyard to let me know what happened after she had begun praying that God would provide $6,000 for her family to take a once-in-a-lifetime trip before the kids grew up and moved out. Prior to the challenge she had determined not to pray for this as she felt it was too selfish of a request. Cindy said that three days earlier she had gone to the mailbox and found a check for exactly $6,000. Apparently, she and her husband had been part of a class action lawsuit and been unexpectedly awarded exactly $6,000. They booked their trip soon after.

These are just two of the hundreds of people who have shared with me since beginning to approach God in bold asking prayer ... since beginning to ask for elephants.[3]

WHAT ARE YOU ASKING FOR?

One thing I have discovered in challenging believers in the area of asking prayer is that few have any specific ideas as to what they are actually praying for. Yes, people pray, but many of their prayers have about as much backbone and structure as a jellyfish. Instead, many Christians pray thematically. Meaning, when they pray, they will say things such as "Dear God, bless my children and keep them loving You and from sin." These are important prayers, prayers that God responds to, but they are not specific.

Specific prayer looks more like this: "Dear God, I pray that You would bless Ruth. I ask that You would surround her with five quality and godly friendships. Remove her fear of failure and help her with telling the truth. I pray she would not lie today and would become the most honest person I have ever known. I pray that she wins the scholastic writing challenge she entered last week."

Do you see the difference? One prayer is broad and shallow; the other has detail and depth. Again, all prayer is important and used by God, but I have experience that specific and strategic prayer has a unique and powerful way of unleashing God's responses in a way generalized prayer does not.

Specificity in prayer is a superhighway for the work of God. We serve a God of detail who dots every i and crosses every t. When we pray in detail, we allow God not only to bless and answer our prayers more effectively but also to demonstrate His love for us in a precise manner.

There is nothing like seeing God provide an answer to a specific request down to the exact penny, precise color, or qualities you are perhaps looking for in the business or perhaps marriage partner of your prayers.

A SEASON OF ANSWERED PRAYER

In the summer of 1998 while I was still a youth pastor at that church in Newport Beach, God challenged me not only to pray specifically but also to keep detailed records of the prayers I prayed.

I decided this because portions of Luke 11 began to spring up everywhere in my life. It was in my daily reading. It was on the radio in my truck, in the sermon I heard on Sunday, and it came up randomly in the conversations I had with friends.

Luke 11 is that chapter where Jesus gave His disciples the scenario of one of them showing up at his friend's house at midnight and specifically asking for three loaves of bread until the owner of the house obliged because of his shameless audacity.

> Then Jesus said to them, "Suppose you have a friend, and you go to him at midnight and say, 'Friend, lend me three loaves of bread; a friend of mine on a journey has come to me, and I have no food to offer him.' And suppose the one inside answers, 'Don't bother me. The door is already locked, and my children and I are in bed. I can't get up and give you anything.' I tell you, even though he will not get up and give you the bread because of friendship, yet because of your *shameless audacity* he will surely get up and give you as much as you need." (Luke 11:5–8)

While God did not specifically direct me in an audible voice to create a list of one hundred detailed prayer requests, that is what I did. You might think that a hundred prayer requests is a lot, but it is actually amazing how quickly you can put together a list like that. Without a tremendous amount of thought, I jotted down prayers in an old journal. I wrote down ten prayers about my marriage, ten about the ministry I oversaw, another ten about my extended family, ten about friends, ten about finances, ten prayers for the sick people I knew, and so on. The final ten prayers on my list were the outlandish ones. These were things like becoming the chaplain for my favorite professional team, a request that has not happened yet, and moving to Australia's Gold Coast for ministry, something we did in 2004.

What happened over the next eighteen months was nothing short of miraculous. God began to answer items on my list immediately. A new sound system was donated to the youth group. It was the exact one I had prayed for down to the model number. I was healed of a nine-millimeter bulging disk in my back that had not allowed me to stand up straight for four months. The day after I was healed, I went for a run and have been fine ever since. Vans, the shoe company, donated a skate park to our church after we prayed for the funds to build one. Kids came to Christ, and one time we earned $28,000 selling fireworks over the Fourth of July weekend, so we did not have to cancel our yearly youth mission trip.

By the end of that year and a half, my list of requests had close to doubled. Trust me, there is nothing like consistent answered prayer to prompt you to ask for more.

The key was that my list never became legalistic. Prayer is more about rhythm than system. There were days when I would just tell God I was too tired to pray, hold up the journal in the air, and ask Him to remember all that was in there. But then there were days when God would nudge me to press in deeper, give a bit of extra thought to a certain prayer, and flesh it out a little more. That's what happened on the day God told me to pray for free rent.

Like many people, your rent or mortgage is probably the largest line item on your monthly expenses. As a newly married youth pastor living in Newport Beach and paying for seminary at the same time, to say things were lean is an understatement. At the time, you could get a pretty good place in Newport Beach for about $1,600. I remember thinking that I was going to challenge God and pray for $800 rent. I would put God to the test.

As I began to pray, a thought came immediately to my mind: *Pray for free rent.* I remember thinking that asking for something like that would show a lack of gratitude toward God. I felt shame in asking God for free rent when there were homeless people in the world. No, I decided that I would not pray that prayer. I would be satisfied with $800 rent.

The problem was that every time I came to the request on my list, this nagging thought would come back into my mind, and now it was saying things such as *When are you going to be obedient and start praying for free rent?* Begrudgingly, I gave in and prayed for free rent.

Not long afterward, I received a call from Concordia University, a school on the border of Newport Beach, asking if Karie and I would be willing to apply for their resident coordinator position. The position not only offered free housing but paid a small salary on top of it. My wife and I jumped at the chance and ended up living and working at Concordia for two years. This is only one example of when God answered beyond the boundary lines I had set down in my personal prayer life. What is even more astonishing is that in the seventeen years Karie and I have been married, we have received free rent for eight of those years. The years at Concordia were just the first two.

THERE'S YOUR ELEPHANT!

About four years after that early morning prayer session with Big Al, I traveled to Bangkok, Thailand, with thirty-eight junior and senior high students. It would be the last of our mission trips that I would lead since I had given my notice a few weeks before the trip. Something was telling me that it was time to move on from Newport Beach.

During the trip, I struggled with whether I had made the right decision. The church had gone through a difficult season starting in my second year, and leaving these kids felt like abandonment to me. Was I doing the right thing? I prayed for confirmation.

On the final night of the trip, I lay on the hard, but thankfully cool, marble floor of the church where we were staying. It was almost midnight when the students finally quieted down.

In the still church, I prayed about my decision and asked God again for confirmation. Just then, and directly after I had prayed for that confirmation, one of the students broke the silence by yelling, "There's an elephant in the courtyard! An elephant is in the courtyard!" We all jumped up and rushed outside. There, in all of its glory, stood a living, breathing elephant.

I remember walking up to the elephant, not recalling the prayer I had prayed with Big Al four years earlier. It was a prayer that had never made it into my top one hundred list. It had always been more of a joke than a real prayer to me. As I reached out my hand, the elephant lifted its moonlit trunk and allowed me to put my fingers on its wet nose. The very moment I touched the elephant, God spoke another thought into my mind: *There's your elephant!* The presence of God was tangible.

I stood in reverent awe gently caressing the animal's trunk and thought, *Are You serious, God? I can't believe it. You gave us our elephant.*

The day God gave me that elephant opened my eyes to the nature of His character. God illustrated not only His extravagance but also His timing and attention to detail. The elephant was the perfect exclamation point to punctuate four years of fantastic ministry while confirming to me that I had made the right decision in moving on. The elephant also showed me that God never forgets a prayer, working them all out to their intended conclusions even after we have forgotten them. But more importantly, the elephant reaffirmed God's deep love for me in a manner far beyond what I could ever have hoped or imagined. In the book of Ephesians Paul said, "Now to him who is able to do far more abundantly than all that we ask or think, according to the power at work within us" (Eph. 3:20 ESV).

Did I need an elephant? No. If God were to have given me a choice of requests to be answered that day, it would not have been for an elephant. There were many things I had asked for in my life that seemed more important in my own understanding. Looking back now as I write this book that I hope will affect countless people's prayer lives and walks with God, I realize that God gave me a bigger elephant than I even prayed for. I just wanted to have fun with kids at a youth group, but God had more global plans for my elephant. The key was having the grace and shameless audacity to pray for one in the first place. For that I credit Big Al.

WHAT'S YOUR ELEPHANT?

The passion and purpose of this book is to help you reignite, re-imagine, and repurpose your prayer life for the sake of knowing God and seeing His kingdom manifested on earth. But this book is also about your elephants. It is about helping you identify through asking prayer the one hundred most important and recklessly outlandish elephants you have the courage to pray for. These are the elephant prayers that if answered by God would be game changers in your life and perhaps the world at large.

Can I assure you God will give you every elephant for which you pray? I cannot. But what I can promise you is that through praying for elephants, you are going to meet and experience the God who loves you deeply.

It's time to start praying for your elephant.

CHAPTER 2

I DARE YOU

Far better is it to dare mighty things, to win glorious triumphs,
even though checkered by failure ... than to rank with those
poor spirits who neither enjoy nor suffer much, because they
live in a gray twilight that knows not victory nor defeat.
—Theodore Roosevelt

A RISKY PROPOSITION

The other day a friend challenged me on this whole asking prayer thing. He said, "Don't you think by writing this book that you are running the risk of leading people on a wild goose chase, where they and the stuff they want become the focus of their spiritual lives?"

Rather than come up with a clever rebuttal, I instead exclaimed, "Absolutely!" As a matter of fact, writing this book was the last thing I wanted to do. I was in the middle of working on a proposal for a book that represented my life's calling when the elephant showed up at my door again.

I fought with God on this book. I was concerned with how it might be perceived and where it might lead. I was concerned about my reputation and being lumped in with those who preach a soft gospel. The only problem was that no matter where I turned, the elephant kept rearing its ugly head, tusk and all. In the end, what I felt like God said was "Are you willing to be misunderstood to do what I am telling you to do?" It's a fair question.

Being misunderstood was something Jesus was truly comfortable with. Whether it was hanging out with prostitutes and drunkards, healing on the Sabbath, or encouraging people to pray for whatever they wanted with the promise that He would answer in the affirmative, it made no difference. Jesus often lived and ministered in a way that caused people concern and raised eyebrows.

Do I think Jesus was concerned that people would misunderstand Him? Yes, I do. While Jesus might have been comfortable with being misunderstood, I don't think He reveled in it. Jesus never wanted people to be hindered in the following of Him exclusively.

With that said, Jesus also was willing to take risks for the purpose of kingdom building. Should Jesus have said instead, "Ask for whatever you want in My name, and if I've got the time, I might get around to it"? No, I think Jesus knew exactly what He was doing when He encouraged His followers to immerse themselves in bold, audacious, and perhaps reckless asking prayer. I believe Jesus knew that bold asking prayer paves the way for profound kingdom living. The following are four scriptural mentions of Jesus's willingness to get into trouble with this reckless promise to answer whatever we are willing to ask for in His name:

Ask, and it will be given to you; seek, and you will find; knock, and it will be opened to you. For everyone who asks receives, and he who seeks finds, and to him who knocks it will be opened. (Matt. 7:7–8 NASB)

And I will do whatever you ask in my name, so that the Father may be glorified in the Son. You may ask me for anything in my name, and I will do it. (John 14:13–14)

If you remain in me and my words remain in you, ask whatever you wish, and it will be done for you. (John 15:7)

You did not choose Me, but I chose you. I appointed you that you should go out and produce fruit and that your fruit should remain, so that whatever you ask the Father in My name, He will give you. (John 15:16 HCSB)

RECKLESS

This was the thing with Jesus. He was always getting into trouble with the spiritual illuminati of the day. Jesus was a bold risk taker who did radical things, but He never did them impetuously. He was a grand and strategic leader whose audacity was never without rhyme or reason. Perhaps the more important question is whether we are willing to meet Jesus's audacity by praying equally audacious prayers.

There are many reasons we tend to hold back on the extravagance of our prayer requests. The most frequent one I encounter is guilt. Whatever the reason, we feel that asking God for what our hearts truly desire will perhaps make Him upset with us. People regularly ask me if they should pray for this or that. Many feel a sense of guilt or shame when it comes to letting God know what is really on their hearts. This was the same thing I felt when God challenged me to pray for the free rent I mentioned in the first chapter.

Guilt is a prayer killer and has no place in your prayer life. I cannot tell you how many answers to prayers I have had after I began to pray boldly when in the past I would not have prayed at all because I felt they were requests that would displease God. For instance, right now I am on a plane sitting in business class at thirty thousand feet. Can I afford business class? No. Would I pay extra for business class even if I had the means to do so? Probably not. I have more strategic ways to spend kingdom money. Am I content to sit in economy class? Yes, with a smile on my face and thanking God that I have the ability to travel at all.

While I am not willing to pay for upgrades on flights, what I *am* willing to do is pray without guilt that my economy seat gets upgraded. This is a prayer I pray every time I fly. For instance, last Sunday, after praying this prayer a few days earlier, a friend stopped me at church and said, "Hey, if you ever fly this particular airline I will get you upgraded as I have lots of miles that expire and I want to bless you." Strangely, it happens to be the exact airline I am flying at this moment somewhere over Kansas eating my hot breakfast with outstretched legs.

I don't really know why God would upgrade my travel arrangements when there are more important issues in the world, nor do I want to guess beyond His love and missional purpose in this little blessing. What I do know is that I got to sit by Sarah. Sarah was a pharmaceutical representative with whom I ended up sharing the gospel. Again, I don't know if this was God or not. What I do know is that **I'm not willing to let guilt herd my requests into dry and waterless pastures.**

REMOVING GUILT FROM PRAYER

Jesus's victory over sin removed not only the consequences of sin but also the guilt, which led to the condemnation in the first place. Condemnation is the natural consequence of guilt. The eighth chapter of Romans tells us there is no longer any condemnation. If there is no condemnation, and condemnation is the result of our guilt, then there should be no guilt either. I'm not saying that God does not convict us, but it is a godly conviction that leads to life rather than useless guilt that leads to death. Many believers would do well to learn the difference. Paul made this clear when he wrote, "Therefore there is now no condemnation for those who are in Christ Jesus" (Rom. 8:1 NASB).

Freedom from condemnation removes guilt. Condemning yourself when guilt no longer exists for the redeemed believer is a choice. If you choose to allow guilt to rule your prayers, it will. Guilt and condemnation are the raw substance of hell. Hell delivers an eternity of condemnation and endless guilt. Daniel said, "And many of them that sleep in the dust of the earth shall awake, some to everlasting life, and some to shame and everlasting contempt" (Dan. 12:2 ASV).

Unfortunately, one of the most prominent places you will find guilt is in the prayer lives of believers. So many believers are ashamed to ask extravagantly or have perhaps stopped praying altogether because they feel that God is mad at them. This is a double win for the Enemy. Either he will keep believers from praying at all, or if they do manage to squeak out a few paltry petitions to God, he will do his best to make sure their prayers never match the grandeur of God's intention for their lives.

I have seen this scenario played out over and over again since I began to lead people in corporate asking prayer events. Take Julie for instance. Julie is a single mother and a friend of mine. Recently, she was able to scrape up the cash to take her daughter on a one-week trip to Florida. This was a huge answer to prayer, as the finances of a working single mom can be tight.

Since Julie and I are friends on social media, I followed all the fun they were having. A day or two before Julie and her daughter were to return home, she posted that while the trip had been really fun, they were a bit disappointed that it had rained every day and they were not going to get to spend a day at the beach. Unfortunately, the next day's weather forecast showed looming and consistent showers.

Feeling what I think was a prompting from the Holy Spirit, I messaged Julie that she should post a prayer request for God to change the weather on the Praying for Your Elephant social media prayer group page. Feeling a bit hesitant, she agreed and posted the request. The next day I awoke to find she had posted pictures of her and her daughter at the beach enjoying warm, bright sunshine.

As expected, I received emails about how I might be misusing asking prayer by indicating that our prayers changed the weather for someone's vacation. It is these types of emails, message board comments, and conversations that frustrate me to no end. I think they frustrate Jesus too. While I appreciate sound theology and apologetics, the God police tend to wear me out. Sometimes it seems as though we spend more time apologizing and trying to explain Jesus's command to ask radically in His name than we do actually praying into it.

We tend to stumble a bit when it comes to believing God might actually do something as extravagant as changing an entire weather pattern just so a mom and her daughter could share a memorable day together. At the same time, had Julie and her daughter been in the path of a major hurricane, we would have had no problem firing up the prayer chain that God might divert the storm for their safety.

Here again is where human understanding might get in the way of effective prayer. We will pray for things like the diversion of a storm if lives are on the line but not be quite so sure to pray in the same direction when only a little girl and her mother's once-in-a-lifetime vacation is on the line. We make God seem small. We assign to Him what we feel is important rather than allowing Him the margin to blow our minds beyond the limits of our understanding.

While I am not claiming our prayers changed the weather for Julie and her daughter, I am also not saying they did not. I do not want to place boundaries on my prayers. **I figure if my prayers are going to have boundaries, they are going to fall somewhere between praying to find my keys and stopping the sun.**

FINDING YOUR KEYS AND STOPPING THE SUN

A few days ago, I was walking out to my car and ran into our church's media guru, Jeffery. Jeffery had been madly searching for his keys when I came upon him. Feeling a nudge in my spirit, I asked Jeffery if he had prayed to find them, to which he said, "No." Feeling really foolish, I stepped out in faith and said, "Let's pray now." Mind you, we were standing in the parking lot at noontime. Within thirty seconds of our amen, Jeffery yelled across the parking lot, "I found them. I found them!"

Here again, as with Julie and the weather, I stood at a crossroads. Did God find Jeffery's keys because we prayed? I have no idea. What I do know is that in both of these instances, the issue was not whether God found the keys or changed the weather but rather God challenging my willingness to pray. Asking prayer is a lot more about willingness to ask than it is whether God decides to respond in the affirmative.

The Bible reveals to us many instances in which people had the willingness to pray for extraordinary events. Whether it was Elijah's prayer to change the rain or Joshua's sun-stopping prayer, the Bible speaks of God answering radical and perhaps even reckless prayers.

The temptation to water down these stories with the argument that these were biblical characters living with power and means that far supersede a modern believer's abilities in Christ is strong. The Bible refutes that argument. In the following verses we see a couple of examples where God has honored the request of normal human beings to do radical and counternatural things. James said, "Elijah was a human being, even as we are. He prayed earnestly that it would not rain, and it did not rain on the land for three and a half years" (James 5:17). And the tenth chapter of Joshua says:

> On the day the LORD gave the Amorites over to Israel, Joshua said to the LORD in the presence of Israel:
> "Sun, stand still over Gibeon,
>   and you, moon, over the Valley of
>   Aijalon."
> So the sun stood still,
>   and the moon stopped,
>   till the nation avenged itself on its
>   enemies,
> as it is written in the Book of Jashar.
> The sun stopped in the middle of the sky and delayed going down about a full day. There has never been a day like it before or since, a day when the LORD listened to a human being. Surely the LORD was fighting for Israel! (Josh. 10:12–14)

Both of these passages make it a point to note that the individuals making such lavish requests of God were mere human beings no different from you or me. The only difference was in their willingness to ask.

BOLD WILLINGNESS

Please note that I am not encouraging you to ask and then run with reckless abandon into what you have prayed for. Asking prayer is not presumption. Asking that God will divert a weather pattern is much different from praying to be able to fly and then jumping off a building. I don't pray for the dissolution of a category five hurricane and then go out for a day sailing, although I might check the weather the next morning with my sailing gear in hand.

Perhaps if the command to pray expectantly for whatever our hearts desire appeared in only one random and obscure verse lodged in between the Minor Prophets and a Bible concordance, I would be less adamant about pursuing relentless, audacious asking prayer.

Here again, take note that I believe in leaving the answers to God. I make no promises as to how God will respond to what we ask. The key is a persistent and pervasive willingness to ask in all areas of our lives. What we don't want to do is bind our prayers according to our own understanding.

When we hold back in prayer, it may be because we lack comprehension of our positional right as sons and daughters of the King. As such, we are fully able, even encouraged, to burst into the throne room of God like a toddler jumping on his or her daddy's lap with all the news of our day and request of the things we desire most and need. Is this not the message of the writer of Hebrews? Paul said, "Let us then with confidence draw near to the throne of grace, that we may receive mercy and find grace to help in time of need" (Heb. 4:16 ESV).

Like Elijah and Joshua, I want to be radical in my asking. I want to see an end to child slavery, cancer, and other horrid trials. I long to see the end of the destruction of the unborn and marriages rescued from the edge of divorce. I want to pray massive, world-changing prayers. At the same time, I want help finding my keys when I lose them. I want it all and more.

I want you to think about the things you pray about. Are your prayers confined by fear, doubt, or perhaps your theology? Is your lack of belief in the way God operates in the world holding back some of the elephants He wants to bring into your life? How expansive are your prayers? Are you willing to take Jesus at His word and pray with godly confidence for absolutely anything in His name?

THEOLOGICAL PRAYER KILLERS

The same friend who challenged me in the beginning of this chapter with a question about leading people astray also told me there were things he would never pray about because of his theological persuasion. For instance, he told me he would never pray for the life of a person if he or she had died in front of him.

This is something I pressed back on. What's the harm in praying for something as long as we understand God is the One who grants or denies these requests? Again, I am in the business of prayer creation; I leave the editorial and distribution responsibilities to God. While I'm not starting a ministry of going to funerals and trying to quicken the spirit of the deceased, are you telling me that if your daughter was hit by a car and slipped away there on the pavement in your arms you would not offer a prayer for God to bring her back?

Yes, I know this takes some of us down a potentially slippery slope of theology. I would be more concerned about this if I were making promises for God. Please note I am not affirming how God will respond to what we pray. But I am saying we should be willing to ask. Cast the spiritual lot.

PRAYING FOR MOTORCYCLES

Last weekend I had the chance to expand the boundaries that confine my prayers. I was off-roading with some friends up in the local mountains when we came across Kevin. Kevin was stranded in the wilderness after his motorcycle had broken down. I felt a nudge in my spirit to ask Kevin to pray for his bike. Ugh. I hate doing things like that, but I equally hate leaving a situation and feeling as though I missed an opportunity to see God move or perhaps see someone saved.

Praying for people's motorcycles brings up all sorts of internal conflicts for me. The first is embarrassment. I don't want people to think I'm a weirdo. The next is my ever-present conflict of faith. Does God really start broken-down motorcycles? I could go on and on. The valid reasons, concerns, and questions about why I should not pray for things like Kevin's motorcycle are abundant.

The best thing to do when you come to an impasse of any kind in your prayer life is simply to pray. So that's what I did. I said to Kevin, "I know this sounds weird, but I am a follower of Jesus who believes that God has the ability to fix your bike if we ask Him. Do you mind if I pray for it?"

Oddly, Kevin was game, and so I laid my hands on the bike and prayed a simple prayer aloud that it would start. It did. Before Kevin rode away, he said how he could not wait to tell all of his friends what had happened. This response from Kevin illustrates part of the threefold mission and purpose of asking prayer mentioned in the previous chapter, specifically that asking prayer proves to the world that we are His disciples. Jesus said, "If you remain in me and my words remain in you, ask whatever you wish, and it will be done for you. This is to my Father's glory, that you bear much fruit, showing yourselves to be my disciples" (John 15:7–8).

If I were to tell you I was comfortable when I prayed for Kevin's bike, I would be lying. I am a human being just like you. I think I even broke out in a little bit of a cold sweat as I prayed for the bike to start. My emotions were a frothing mix of hope that God would move, fear that He would not, and embarrassment for being the dude who prays for motorcycles to start.

These are the types of experiences you might have if you start to pray beyond your boundaries. No, I am not promising that every motorcycle you pray for will start, but a lot more might start than the ones you did not pray for. I can assure you of that.

JESUS SUCKER PUNCH

At the beginning of this chapter, I affirmed Jesus's willingness to be misunderstood. The problem is that most people still misunderstand the real tension of Jesus's statements on asking prayer. I believe that the tension here is not so much if Jesus will answer everything we pray for, but rather if we are actually willing to ask for more than we might want. Read that sentence again.

Here's what I mean. In case you missed it, Jesus did not just encourage His listeners to ask for whatever they desired; He also beseeched them to ask for anything. He said, "And I will do whatever you ask in my name, so that the Father may be glorified in the Son. You may ask me for *anything* in my name, and I will do it" (John 14:13–14).

Jesus's theology of asking prayer seems alluring at first, even exciting. Christ woos His hearers in with grand promises of rewarding their deepest desires. This is a promise He intends to keep provided that certain criteria are in play. Then without warning, once we are hooked on visions of our grandeur, success, or personal happiness, comes the sucker punch. If you are not familiar with that term, it is a phrase associated with fighting. It means throwing an unexpected punch, usually to the gut, that your opponent never sees coming and that buckles the opponent's knees.

If you don't want to be caught off guard by Jesus, then you need to understand what He said in its original language and context. Like English, the ancient Greek language has words with multiple meanings. One of these words is *thelō*. It is a word used 213 times in the New Testament in its various forms.[1] *Thelō* is a word that can be translated as "wishes" or "desires," and in some translations of the Bible it has been. But a more expansive understanding of the word is "willing" or perhaps "willingness." We find this stiff uppercut of a word in many biblical passages. For instance, Jesus said, "If ye abide in me, and my words abide in you, *ye shall ask what ye will* [*thelō*], and it shall be done unto you" (John 15:7 KJV).

Many modern translations use words like "whatever you desire" or "whatever you wish" when translating *thelō* in John 15:7.[2] When we look at less recent translations,[3] we see that the emphasis rests on willingness rather than personal desire. Here again, it seems that the older translations have a more expansive understanding of what

Christ is getting at. It seems Jesus is challenging us to ask for more than we just want or wish; He is daring us to ask for whatever we might be willing to ask for.

Another place the word *thelō* is used with this broader understanding is in John 7:17. Here the NIV translation chooses to translate the same word *thelō* as an individual choosing rather than what a person wants or desires. Jesus said, "Anyone who chooses [*thelō*] to do the will of God will find out whether my teaching comes from God or whether I speak on my own" (John 7:17).

From my personal studies, I feel that many newer translations miss the fullness of this word's intent when dealing with the Christ message of asking prayer, and I tend to agree with the translation of the King James Version when dealing with John 15:7. The point is that asking prayer is just as much about asking for what we want as for what we might not want but are willing to ask for courageously. Humility might be a request that falls into this category. That we might experience the fellowship of His suffering might be another. (See Phil. 3:10.)

While Jesus takes pleasure in giving us the things we want, we mustn't see our changing wants as the fulcrum of Christ's teaching on bold asking prayer. What we want is so limited, so feeble, so minute. It is limited to what we can comprehend about our own desires. It is limited to us.

Jesus expands the boundaries of asking prayer. He is daring you to ask beyond your wants. Imagine how frail this immense teaching would be if we were promised answers only to the things we could conjure up within our own desires. What you want has limitations. On the other hand, having a willingness to pray boldly for anything has no boundaries and might include a prayer such as "Jesus, what do You want from me?" This is a prayer we might tend to extricate from our prayers if they include only our desires. This is because many of the things Jesus might ask of us probably would not be things we would want or desire.

Again, Jesus knew that if He only implored us to ask for what we wanted, we would be forced to live within the emaciated confines of our own understanding. If you are only allowed to ask for what you want, then you will never be able to ask for what you don't want or what you don't understand.

Challenging His followers to ask for anything is a much more dangerous offer to His disciples than challenging them to ask for whatever they might want in that moment. This is absolutely crucial to your understanding of the message of the elephant and the message of Christ. Yes, Jesus wants you to ask for what you want, but He is also challenging you far beyond that. Jesus is daring you to pray for things you might not want. This might mean praying for the ability to forgive the ex-husband who cheated on you with your best friend or perhaps the courage to give away 50 percent of your life savings to missions. As I said, Jesus did not just say ask for what you want; He said ask for anything you are willing to ask for. It's much more difficult to get infatuated with this statement by Jesus when we see it in full context.

ARE YOU WILLING?

As we go forward in praying for your elephants, I want to challenge you with *thelō*. As Christ did, I want to dare you to ask for not just what you want but, more importantly, what you are willing to ask. I want you to expand the territory of your prayers far beyond the slim boundaries of only what you want and explore the vast and uncharted territory of what God wants for you. This means the willingness to ask God to ask anything of you. Is it not fair that if God is willing to do whatever we ask of Him that we might offer the same in return? Like the example of Jesus in the garden, He was willing to ask for both what He wanted and what He might not. Jesus said, "Father, if thou be willing, remove this cup from me: nevertheless not my will, but thine, be done" (Luke 22:42 KJV).

This is courageous prayer, selfless prayer, prayer that brings kingdoms and releases herds of unknown elephants into your life. This is the dare of Jesus. Will you take it?

CHAPTER 3

IDENTIFYING YOUR ELEPHANTS

*Prayer does the salvage work of raising the
sunken treasure of our lives.*

FREE-RUNNING

I said in chapter 1 that few believers have any idea of what they
are actually praying for. Granted, they know the major themes of
their prayers—themes like family, work, friends, health, and perhaps
a few specific requests such as a raise or class placement for their
kindergartner—but if you were to ask them to describe in detail and
specificity the exact nature of their individual prayers, it would be a
short conversation. This is because many of us have become accus-
tomed to "free-running" our prayer lives.

Back when I attended Point Loma Nazarene University, I had
this friend from Alaska named Wes. Wes drove a Subaru, smoked,

listened to Tom Waits, and was the one who told me about free-running. People from Alaska intrigue me. Wes was no exception. According to Wes, scientists back in the sixties performed experiments with people's sleep cycles. They would put volunteers in windowless rooms while keeping the lights continually burning. They would give volunteers undergoing the experiment no indication as to the time of day or any hints of rhythm by which their internal body clocks or circadian rhythms could attune. According to my Alaskan friend Wes, scientists discovered that the participants had wildly sporadic sleeping cycles. They would do things like stay up a day at a time, sleep two hours, and then stay up another six hours before hitting the sack for fifteen hours straight. They had completely lost their internal understanding of life's cadence. In regard to the natural rhythmic order of this world, they had no compass.

While I have not seen Wes since we shared a dorm together in the early nineties, I've never forgotten this story. My wife and I actually refer to it when we feel our calendar or perhaps finances have gotten out of control. Usually, one of us will say, "We need to stop free-running our finances." We immediately know what the other means. We know it's time to again lay foundational structure to our lives. We need consistency.

When we free-run our prayer lives for too long, we also can lose our sense of God's rhythm and action, as the ebb and flow of strategic prayer act as a beacon for daily living. As you experience God responding to specific requests, you become aware of what He is actually doing in your life and the world. In essence, prayer becomes a spiritual sun and your moon, informing you of the movements and rhythm of God around you.

RESPONDING TO OUR PRAYERS

I use the word *respond* to prayers rather than *answer* to prayers for a purpose. For me and perhaps many others, the thought of having prayers answered connotes the idea of God saying yes, no, or perhaps wait. This is not to say that I won't refer to God's responses as answers throughout this book, but rather I have a more holistic view of how God treats requests.

What I have found is that God's responses to my prayers are often multifaceted rather than simple monosyllabic answers of yea or nay. For instance, sometimes I don't get an answer to a direct request but instead a deep emotional feeling about the situation. Oftentimes these emotional promptings create a state of emotional, spiritual, and mental well-being around a certain request that frames it in a completely different light and in the process changes me.

Even if an individual prayer goes rogue and never seems to find a direct answer, that feeling or sense given by the Holy Spirit gives me peace beyond having to receive a decisive or conclusive answer. Finding contentment in God's responses rather than His direct answers is a sign of spiritual maturity. (See Phil. 4:10–13.)

What I have also discovered is that if God only gave me what I wanted, I would miss out on so much more that He might want to do. As limited human beings, we tend to focus on the solidarity of the thing we are asking for. God on the other hand sees the eternal landscape that each prayer offers Him. We pray a single prayer for a momentary blessing, but God sees the opportunity to turn that prayer into something far beyond the confines of our limited understanding. What God did with my prayer for an elephant has far surpassed momentarily wowing some kids at a youth group event. God's ability to respond far beyond what we ask is one of the things that makes prayer spiritually nuclear. Each prayer is an atom that if split by God has unending possibilities.

I call these prolific responses by God the tailwind of prayer. The basic concept is that a single prayer often has the ability to achieve more than you ever imagined. Prayer has a way of blowing wind into other sails in your life that you might not even be praying about.

Think about it this way. My mom is a classically trained chef. She and my father opened many restaurants together. Often I'll ask my mom if she will make one of her special dishes. When it's time to eat, I find that my mother has made not only what I asked for but things I have not asked for that complement what I requested. Not only is there an amazing beef Wellington, but she has garnished it with potatoes au gratin, asparagus, and a Caesar salad—all this before we even get to dessert.

When I pray in specific and strategic ways, God prepares a meal of response that far exceeds what I even considered. I only want a ham sandwich, but God leads me to a buffet.

Let me again highlight Ephesians 3:20, with a special emphasis on God being able to do far more than you could ever think or ask. In its most blunt terms, I believe this verse promises that you could spend an eternity conjuring up the wildest and most eccentric prayer requests and still fall far short of what God has planned for you.

David understood the concept of God's buffet and expressed it in a profound way in Psalm 23. David, a man committed to bold asking prayer, said, "You serve me a six-course dinner right in front of my enemies. You revive my drooping head; my cup brims with blessing. Your beauty and love chase after me every day of my life" (Ps. 23:5–6 MSG).

When I free-run my prayer life, I am completely unaware of this tailwind and buffet of God's responses, presence, and grand drama in my life. Free-running prayer is something I have done for a long time. Yes, there have been many seasons when I had a regular, specific, and strategic prayer life, but my proclivity to drift off into unstructured and nonspecific free-running prayer is incredibly strong.

Before the legalism police among us shout, "What about grace?" slow down before you choke on your God whistle. Let me affirm that it is impossible to pray without grace. I dare not think what would happen if I approached God's throne for any reason without the grace of divine invitation and a position of heir. As I remember from my Old Testament studies, it did not go so well for those who tried.

What I am talking about is structured determination, not some legalistic form of prayer that binds and chains us. What I am advocating is more strategic rhythm than system. I have no desire to put heavy burdens on those who read this book. With that said, I do believe that if a person prays in a legalistic fashion, it is still far better than no prayer at all. At least God has something to work with. What I have discovered is that **it is easy to cast aside spiritual discipline and label it legalism to gratify our inner sloth.** I have also discovered that consistent, undisciplined prayer in the name of grace can easily become a form of passive legalism. Isn't legalism the adherence to a system of law? We can just as easily be committed to prayerlessness in a legalistic manner as we can to dogmatic systems of prayer. This consistent prayerlessness in the name of grace becomes the legalism of inaction.

PASTOR ORVILLE'S TABLET

Pastor Orville Stanton is one of my favorite people I have worked with. Orville came to Christ in the sixties as a hippie, lived in a commune with his wife for years, eats his own garden's organically grown produce, and at sixty-six years of age is strong as an ox. Incrementally, he is hiking the entire 2,663-mile Pacific Crest Trail from the northern border of Mexico to the southern boundary line of Canada.

Orville is not only a man of God, he is also a man of deep, regular, and specific asking prayer. He has this habit of carrying a little notepad in his hip pocket wherever he goes. If you are ever speaking with Orville and mention something that might need prayer, perhaps a sick relative or the need for tickets to an event for your upcoming anniversary, Orville reaches into his pocket for a little tattered notepad. If you were to look closely, you would see that Orville's notepad is inundated with precise notes about the things he is praying for.

In a way, this compilation of jotted-down prayers is a living history of what God has done and is doing in Orville's life and the lives of others who surround him. When Orville says he is going to pray for you, he means it. He never uses Christian etiquette to politely exit a conversation. Each week in our Wednesday pastors' prayer time, he pulls out his little prayer tablet. When it comes time for him to pray, you will hear the little pages flip as he rattles off continued petition for items still in play and thanksgiving for those that have been responded to by God. Orville does not free-run his prayer life. If you were to sit down to coffee with Orville and ask him what he is praying about, you would be in for a robust conversation on where God is walking on the trails, valleys, and peaks of his life.

What about you? Are you currently free-running your prayer life? If someone were to ask you what you are actually praying about, would you have much to say? These questions are not intended to induce guilt. Rather, they are meant for the purpose of encouraging you to take a look at your prayer life. The hope is that you begin to develop a strategic group of asking prayers that unlock God's future and purposes for your mission here on earth.

SUNKEN TREASURE

The book of James says, "You do not have because you do not ask" (James 4:2). To illustrate this scripture, let me tell you a story I once heard about a little boy who had a dream of heaven. In the dream, God took the boy to a room. In the room were various types of material possessions like cars, houses, and other objects needed for daily life. Also in the room were things that seemed grotesque: eyeballs, legs, hands, and feet piled high in various corners. When the little boy asked God what it all meant, God replied, "These are answers to prayers never prayed."

Whether or not this boy went to heaven is not really important to me. Even if the story is fictional, it still carries a profound message. The moral of this story is scripturally accurate. People do not possess many of the things God intends for their lives for one simple reason: they have never asked.

While I understand concerns that surface about God's sovereignty when a verse such as James 4:2 is read, I believe that we need to take it at face value. Like sunken treasure littering the bottom of the sea, God's responses to unprayed prayers are left undiscovered and lost.

What about you? Is some of the treasure of your life resting with the Spanish galleons deep below your life's surface and waiting for the salvage work of prayer to excavate them? Are you perhaps missing out on what God intends for your life because you have never asked?

I think this is true for all of us. If God has more for us than we could ever ask for or imagine, then we all have some slack in our lines. (See Eph. 3:20.) How much of that slack we rein in is up to our determination in asking prayer and, of course, God's grace.

PRAYERFUL IMAGINATION

One of the problems with sunken treasure is that it is often not where you think it is. The same is true with asking prayer. The issue is not people's ability to pray but rather a lack of Spirit-guided imagination leading you toward the treasure trove of what God desires. **Spirit-led imagination is the fuel of prayer creation.** Few believers spend much time doing the difficult work of imagining what their lives or world could look like beyond their current experience. Many focus on the failures of the past and fears of the future rather than redeeming the past and changing the future by asking in prayer.

For example, let's say your son or daughter struggles with drug addiction. Many will pray for sobriety but fail to spend much time imagining what their child's life could look like once sober and then praying for that. Rather than praying for freedom from addiction, you can also imagine and pray for a life free of substance abuse. You can pray for your child's career, dreams, spouse, kids, etc. Because of the work of prayerful imagination, you are able to pray far beyond the current circumstances. Few people do this. The tyranny of the momentary crisis often robs us of prayerful, futuristic, Spirit-led imagining.

When it comes to imagination, two cultural icons immediately come to mind. The first is Walt Disney, and the other is Steve Jobs. Both of these men had the ability to see light-years beyond their contemporaries. Both were hard-driving workers. More importantly, both valued imagination as a key component to life and business success.

Disney and Jobs were men who spent as much time in the realm of imagination as they did actually putting the results of those imaginations to work.

For instance, when Disney was near bankruptcy, instead of going out and looking for financing, a task he often left to his brother Roy, he sat with his drawing pad imagining. What he imagined that day changed the world. Walt Disney said, "Mickey Mouse popped out of my mind onto a drawing pad twenty years ago on a train ride from Manhattan to Hollywood at a time when business fortunes of my brother Roy and myself were at lowest ebb and disaster seemed right around the corner."[1]

I love how Disney said that Mickey Mouse popped out of his mind. The thing that would change not only his life but the entire world just popped out of his mind while riding on the train. Is it possible that if we spent time in prayerful imagination that the elephants that will change our lives might just pop out of our minds and souls too? I know they can.

Steve Jobs talked about the creativity of imagination like this: "Creativity is just connecting things. When you ask creative people how they did something, they feel a little guilty because they didn't really *do* it, they just *saw* something. It seemed obvious to them after a while. That's because they were able to connect experiences they've had and synthesize new things."[2]

If you take anything onboard from this chapter, take this: prayer is just as much about imagination as it is actually fashioning those imaginations into concrete prayer requests. Understanding this concept was a huge breakthrough for me. Before I understood this, I used to feel that specific and strategic prayer requests would just appear out of thin air while I was praying. Sometimes they did, but as you can imagine, they often did not and I would consistently depart from my times of prayer feeling discouraged.

These days, I spend as much time in prayerful imagining as I do actually praying the specific, strategic, and concrete prayers I created through imagining with God. Sometimes I will spend an entire hour just trying to imagine deeper into my elephant prayer list. When I come to the section dedicated to my marriage, I ask God to help me reimagine that portion of my list and life. I think about new things I can pray for that would bless my wife and me as a couple. I imaginatively explore ten years from now. I think about the places we might visit, the depth of love we might possess, ministry adventures, and a family culture that makes Jesus central.

Eventually, I make my way to the category representing my daughter's school. Here I imagine what the most dynamic,

Christ-centered public school experience could look like. I imagine the kind of friends Jesus would want her to have. I imagine her in on-campus ministry. I imagine her succeeding in her educational pursuits. I conjure thoughts of what it would be like if she did not just know about God but knew Him as her heavenly Father. I try my best to out-imagine God. Thankfully, through the counsel of the Holy Spirit, I have a collaborator in the creativity of my soulful imagination.

Let me assure you that doing this is not always easy. Prayer is a labor of love. The work of imagination is hard, and oftentimes I sit for long periods without scribbling down a word. But then there are those other times when something comes to mind that if God answered would be a game changer. I hear an elephant in the brush. It is when this happens that I go back to the work of consistently praying it through. I add it to my list. This is how imagination expands our prayers and releases God's purposes and desires into our lives. How big is your imagination? Would Walt Disney or Steve Jobs look at your prayers and say, "Wow, you know how to dream"?

NOT A BOOK ABOUT PRAYER

This book is not a book about prayer but rather a book that asks you to pray. There is a big difference between books about prayer and books that jump-start your prayer life. I can't tell you how many amazing books I have read on prayer and then never prayed. It's almost as though reading a book about prayer releases the tension enough to continue the prayerless life free of guilt. Perhaps you know what I mean. That is why I have done my best to create a resource where the pages come alive as you pray your way through this book. If you have not begun to pray by this chapter, I want to challenge you to begin the Praying for Your Elephant prayer journey.

Like Orville's mighty journey along the Pacific Crest Trail, every great expedition starts with a humble first step. The first step in this journey is to take the time to identify your elephants through determined, Spirit-led, imaginative asking prayer.

I want to challenge you to create a list of your one hundred elephant requests. Granted, a hundred requests might seem like a lofty goal, but if you compare it to our other desires, it's really not so grand a proposition. For instance, if I told people that a private billionaire financier was willing to pay for their top one hundred material requests, it would not take too long to fashion that list. It's really a matter of what we value.

While prayer is not a gumball machine that pumps out answers to requests after receiving your quarter, it is governed by the God of the universe who delights in responding to the requests of His children. If you take this challenge seriously and assault heaven with your imaginative, specific, and strategic requests, God will respond. If you nurture these prayers, they will create a subtle breeze in you that will release a furious storm of God in and around your life. If you take this challenge, get ready to batten down the hatches.

HOW TO CAPTURE
AN ELEPHANT

Hi Pastor Adam,

Here's the paperweight elephant I got you, all the way from Kenya! Let me explain.

As a child, my parents were very involved in church. When missionaries would speak at our church, they would often stay at our house. I remember sitting up late and hearing the fantastical stories.

On one of these occasions, a missionary gave me a handmade Bible bookmark. On the bookmark was the word DALAT. The missionary explained to me that this was the name of a school for missionary kids. Right then, at five years old, I knew I would be a teacher, but I also thought I would be a teacher at a missionary school. Ever since I have had a deep desire to get on the missions field, but the timing never seemed right.

On March 10th I went to the short-term missions meeting at church and immediately felt drawn to Kenya. This was a couple of weeks after you had told the story about your elephant. I decided to start praying for mine. *I had wanted this elephant for so long. I talked to Tom (husband) about it, and he understandably asked, "How much is it?" When I told him it was between $3,100 and $3,200 he told me what I already knew, saying, "Babe, you know you are on unpaid leave right now. I know you will go sometime, but now is just not that time."*

So I just started praying for my elephant with reckless abandon. I prayed every day. I just could not get Kenya off my mind. My prayer was, "Lord, either shelve this desire for now or work it out."

On the twelfth day of praying for my elephant, I got a call from the district office. They said, "We have a paycheck for you. You need to come down and get it." I explained there must be a mistake, I'm on unpaid leave, etc. She double-checked and confirmed all of that to be true, but said that if I did not come and get the check it would be redistributed as summer pay at a later date. I drove to the school praying the entire way. I opened the envelope and found a check for $3,137.

Almost forty years later, I got my elephant. I knew I had to buy you one when I was in Kenya.

God bless,
Jana

CHAPTER 4

LOST IN SPACE

When faith ceases to pray, it ceases to live.

—E. M. Bounds

PREPARING TO LAUNCH

Prayer is a launchpad that will thrust your life into eternal reality. The problem is, shortly after liftoff, it's easy to feel lost in space. Like an astronaut who is separated from the mother ship and spinning out of control toward the sun, prayer can also cause us to feel helpless and somewhat lost.

My attempts at relaunching my prayer life always start with the best of intentions. Usually I have been at a conference or church service where someone has spoken on prayer. I get excited and decide that I am going to take prayer seriously again. It usually looks like this:

My alarm crows at 5:30 a.m. I've set it with the best of intentions. By 5:50 a.m., my wife is kicking me and telling me to either get up or turn the snooze feature to mute. I stumble out of bed. The route to the coffeemaker is a well-trodden path.

Grind beans. Pour water. Press percolate.

Rather than jumping right into prayer by quieting my heart, I decide it would be a good idea to check my email. Before the coffee is brewed, I have not only reviewed last night's scores, but I've also priced a flight for an imaginary trip I will probably never take.

If I can't find my favorite mug, I have to search all over the house. This takes another five or ten minutes. Granted, there are other perfectly good mugs, but I need my special one. Jesus had His Holy Grail. I have my mug. It's biblical.

Now it's 6:20ish and the kids are starting to stir. I slip into the office, close the door, and nestle into my prayer chair. If you don't have a prayer chair, I highly encourage you to search one out.

At this point I try to quiet my mind, but random thoughts jump around in my head like a thousand wild monkeys hopped up on bananas. I try to focus and start by praying for my wife. Before I get halfway through the first sentence, I think, *You forgot to confess your sins.* I stop praying for my wife and dredge up a laundry list of things I need to accept forgiveness for. Less than a minute into that list, I remember I should have started with adoration. I learned this as a kid in Sunday school. Perhaps you remember the ACTS acronym to remind us of the supposed proper order of a prayer time. It stands for adoration, confession, thanksgiving, and supplication. Even though I've always questioned "systems" of prayer, I do it anyway. I figure it's better than nothing. I cease with the confession I started and try to praise God. Now I'm searching my mental Rolodex for songs to sing to God.

Suddenly, I get this brilliant thought that my prayer time would be much improved if I had some praise music to accompany me. I stop praying and start looking for my giant headphones. More time goes by. It's getting close to 7:00 a.m. now, and the kids are banging on the door. It's okay, though. They're not interrupting me. I've been on iTunes buying worship music for the last twenty minutes. It's time to get up and go to work.

Sound familiar?

EXPERTS IN PRAYER

I've always wanted to be an expert in prayer. People such as Saint Francis of Assisi, Teresa of Avila, my friend Andy from England, or Brother Lawrence with his continual practicing of the presence of God amaze and inspire me. These prayer aficionados all have amazing stories of what God did when they began to pray. As a matter of fact, some historic Christians were so good at prayer, you can go down to your local garden store and get stone statues of them to put in your yard. Just think, maybe one day if you get really good at prayer, you will be in lots of people's gardens too. My problem is I stink at prayer. Maybe it's because I am an extrovert with ADHD.

My wife is good at prayer, much better than I am. She's an introvert. Introversion in my opinion is like steroids for prayer. I think this is an unfair advantage and should be regulated better by God. My wife, Karie, likes to sit quietly for hours with her Bible on her lap talking to God. She is much closer to being a perch for birds in your yard than I am.

However, when we begin to rate our prayer times or see other people as spiritual experts with résumés and exploits that we can never attain, we again are navigating the ships of our spiritual lives off course. The seas of prayer have no experts, no professionals. Rather, expertise is exchanged for bold humility.

Back at Point Loma Nazarene University, I had this professor named Dr. Paul Orajala.[1] Paul was a gentle man who always had a word of encouragement or wisdom for me when I was in a pinch. Once when struggling with my prayer life, I went to Dr. O's office for some counsel. He said, "Adam, there are no experts in prayer. Prayer is an eternal commodity. How can any mortal be an expert in eternity? If anyone tells you that they are an expert in prayer, run!"

What Dr. O said was actually a word of grace that deconstructs systems of achievement. These systems can become heavy burdens on people and cause them to live under the cloak of guilt and shame if they fail to keep up or hit the mark.

Another believer by the name of Paul also put forth the premise that there are no experts in prayer or any other spiritual exercise. The apostle Paul wrote in his letter to the Romans, "In the same way the Spirit also helps *our weakness; for we do not know how to pray as we should*, but the Spirit Himself intercedes for us with groaning too deep for words" (Rom. 8:26 NASB).

Here Paul said that the starting place of every prayer is from a position of weakness. No one knows how he or she ought to pray. This includes some of the most dedicated people of prayer whom the world and heaven have ever known. Like the rest of us, the genesis of prayer begins from the same posture of dependence and weakness. Prayer is always a subordinate approaching a sovereign. What gives prayer its power and effectiveness is less about the people who pray or the system of prayer they use, but rather God the Father who delights in turning His children's weakness into great strength.

It is from this platform and reality of weakness that our prayers gain their strength and efficacy. As our prayers travel from the launchpads of our hearts into the deep space that is God's being, they are transformed and made powerful. Paul touted this weakness as the believer's strength. He said, "Therefore I am well content with weaknesses, with insults, with distresses, with persecutions, with difficulties, for Christ's sake; for when I am weak, then I am strong" (2 Cor. 12:10 NASB).

While this verse is not specifically addressing prayer, it is not poor biblical interpretation to say that Paul saw weakness as the starting point for all spiritual discipline. This includes prayer. Paul was a man who had no confidence in his flesh or ability but was completely dependent on God. In Paul's letter to the Galatians, he said, "I have been crucified with Christ. It is no longer I who live, but Christ who lives in me. And the life I now live in the flesh I live by faith in the Son of God, who loved me and gave himself for me" (Gal. 2:20 ESV).

EMBRACING WEAKNESS AS STRENGTH

Embracing weakness as strength is a key premise on which the message of the elephant rides. I cannot express how important this understanding is in regard to becoming a person who is dedicated to prayer. So often the self-awareness of our own weakness in the discipline of prayer becomes the very thing that makes us stumble rather than relying on it to be our strength. Many believers, myself included, have stalled along the pilgrimage of prayer because of these deep feelings of inadequacy and ineffectiveness.

This is one of the betting tables that the Devil regularly cashes in on. He is laying a wager that you will believe something anti-scriptural, namely that there are experts in prayer. If you buy into his lie, then consequently you believe there are novices in prayer as well.

Scripture affirms that you will never be anything but a novice at prayer. (See Rom. 8:26.) As a matter of fact, *novice* is too lofty of a word. Rather, we are infants fresh from the womb and completely dependent on our parent God to provide, strengthen, and nourish our prayers. We babble our nonsensical cries into God's deep space, and He receives them with great anticipation and joy.

If you feel hopeless in prayer because of your weakness, then you are just where God wants you. The weaker, more lost, and more desperate you feel, the stronger you are. This is the confidence we have in weakness.

This is what Dr. Orajala was telling me back in the early nineties. He was warning me to never seek expertise in prayer, to never feel as if I was more than a pilgrim along the way.

EXPERIENCE OVER EXPERTISE

Think again about the astronaut I mentioned at the beginning of the chapter. Like us when it comes to prayer, no one is an expert when it comes to space. How can you become an expert at something that you will never have more than a minimal understanding of? All you have to do to prove an astronaut's ignorance is ask him or her one simple question, "How big is space?" You can go to the moon a million times and never be able to answer that question.

How about asking NASA this question: "Where are we?" Yes, they could tell you where we are in relation to other objects like the sun, but if they have no idea as to the actual size of space, then how can they know where we actually are? If you can't tell me how big space is or where we are, then your expertise is limited. Would you get in a car with someone who had this limited understanding of where he or she was going? If so, be prepared to drive around in circles for days.

While astronauts will never be true space experts, what they can do is experience space in a rich and meaningful way. This is true for us in the limitless landscape of prayer. While you will never be an expert in the eternal space that is prayer, you can experience it in significant ways.

Having been to space, Neil Armstrong could have told me things about it that I will never understand unless I also venture there to experience it myself. Through experiencing space, Armstrong had a perspective few people on this planet will ever have. He knew what the world looked like from afar. He felt the heat of the sun unencumbered by earth's ozone layer, stepped on the moon's surface, and saw galaxies from the universe's front row. While Armstrong might never have been an expert, who would not want to trade experiences with him if they could?

Like Armstrong with space, you can experience prayer's vast expanses in vibrant and profound ways. Perhaps the only thing holding you back is your willingness to suit up and launch, fully cognizant of your weakness. Paul said, "But he said to me, 'My grace is sufficient for you, for my power is made perfect in weakness.'

Therefore I will boast all the more gladly of my weaknesses, so that the power of Christ may rest upon me" (2 Cor. 12:9 ESV).

Now that we have a firm understanding of our weakness, let's take a look at how this weakness is transformed into our great strength.

MADE IN TRANSLATION

My wife and I are Anglophiles. We love all things English. Not only do we do our best to spend as much time in the UK as possible, but our home is full of British pictures, literature, and knickknacks from our travels. Often when the girls get home from a hard day at school, we have our own version of British low tea, complete with sticky date pudding or clotted cream and scones. Sometimes we even put on faux accents. Yes, I understand we are nerds.

When it comes to date night, forget about Superman or whatever other action movie is playing in the theaters. We are suckers for British period pieces. I can't tell you how many times we've watched *Persuasion* or *Pride and Prejudice*. I might as well wear a top hat and go by the moniker Mr. Darcy.

No matter how many times we go to the UK or other commonwealth constituents around the globe, I am reminded of how different we still are. It's surprising that we can all speak the same language, but our words can mean so many different things. Our *bathrooms* are called their *loos*. *Police officers* in America are known as *bobbies* in London and Manchester. While Americans want to do something *right*, Britons prefer it to be done *proper*.

I can't tell you how many times I have said something in mixed British company only to have people look shocked or start laughing hysterically. What I meant to express obviously was not what was understood. The meaning had been lost in translation.

The *Urban Dictionary* defines "lost in translation" as follows: "When something is translated into another language, and sometimes translated back into the original language, and because of differences of the languages some of the original meaning is lost."[2]

This never happens when you pray. You are never the butt of angels' jokes when you offer up petitions to God in their presence. On the contrary, when we pray, the Holy Spirit sorts out our feeble and mixed-up prayers as they make the short journey from the material world into the ethereal one. This is because when we pray, the meaning is made understandable in translation.

Here again, in Romans 8:26–28, we see a powerful truth about God's ability to turn our weakness into great strength. I love how Eugene Peterson presented this verse in *The Message* version of the Bible:

> Meanwhile, the moment we get tired in the waiting, God's Spirit is right alongside helping us along. If we don't know how or what to pray, it doesn't matter. He does our praying in and for us, making prayer out of our wordless sighs, our aching groans. He knows us far better than we know ourselves, knows our pregnant condition, and keeps us present before God. That's why we can be so sure that every detail in our lives of love for God is worked into something good. (Rom. 8:26–28 MSG)

Let's dig into those verses. As we pray, the Holy Spirit is always there acting as our copetitioner before the throne of God. This means that each time you pray, you do not pray alone. Imagine if most believers accepted this as truth when they prayed. How would this understanding change the way we pray? Would it not breed ultimate confidence in that particular prayer time's ultimate power and purpose?

Peterson used the word *if* in the phrase "If we don't know how or what to pray." I would say a word truer to the original text would be *because*: "Because we don't know how or what to pray."[3] I determine this by Paul's use of the perfect tense, which disqualifies the use of *if* in my opinion. Regardless, the point of the text is that God's Spirit commandeers every prayer we pray in a form of spiritual mutiny. We do our best attempt to create passion and purpose-filled prayers, and then the Holy Spirit says, "I'll take the helm from here."

Once the Holy Spirit captains our prayers, He goes about the work of reconstituting those prayers from things like improper motive, limited understanding of what is actually good for us, and pride. He then presents these confessions, thanksgivings, and supplications to God the Father as perfect before filling the sails of these prayers with the wind and power of His Spirit.

This is why it is absolutely ridiculous when believers make statements about their inability to pray eloquently or put other believers on a pedestal because of their proficiency with language. Prayer is more than just words. Prayer is a heart and soul groaning, not an exercise in vocabulary for the purpose of impressing others.

I need to walk the tightrope of truth here, because I believe that the words we craft and use when praying have important purposes in opening strategic doors in our lives. At the same time I want to assert that no matter what words you choose in your own limited understanding to pray, they still need to be deconstructed and then reconstructed by the Holy Spirit before they are ready to be presented to God's throne in perfection. This is why a heartfelt, faith-filled, one-word prayer by a four-year-old child has the ability to cataclysmically rumble through heaven in a more dynamic way than perhaps some "professional" Christian's rehearsed, theatrical, and dramatic tent-meeting prayer meant only to impress has.

Because of the Holy Spirit's gift of translation, it is impossible for any heartfelt prayer to arrive at the doorstep of heaven in a state of imperfection. Here again, the burden of prayer's perfection is not entrusted into the hands of the one praying but rather to the Holy Spirit, the great fixer of our prayers. As Peterson said, the Holy Spirit does our praying for us. This is why the greatest obstacle to a powerful life of prayer is not the words you use but simply failing to say anything at all. This would be what you would call a failure to launch.

FAILURE TO LAUNCH

I will never forget where I was on January 28, 1986. I was in the tenth grade then and serving an all-day in-school suspension for some caper I had failed to pull off. Around 11:15 in the morning I was summoned to the principal's office. I was thinking, *What did I do now? How do you get busted when you are already in detention?*

When I arrived, the office was in a kind of weird, melancholy panic. People were standing around looking shocked. Someone tuned a radio to the local news station. The space shuttle *Challenger* had imploded just after liftoff. I was summoned in to break the news to all the classes.

I remember how I felt that day. Even as a kid who had no real connection to anyone on that mission, I was emotionally affected in a profound way. We all were. Looking back, I think this had something to do with how previous generations and mine viewed space exploration and the adventurous few who were willing to explore this final frontier.

While successive generations' interest in the continued exploration of space has waned, this was not the case shortly after the tragedy. On the contrary, there seemed to be a renewed constitution that this setback would not discourage us from continuing to launch.

PUSH THE BUTTON

While you can spend all the time in the world preparing to launch, you will never blast off until you eventually push the button. Regardless of your previous prayer experiences, whether dramatic successes or epic failures, the key is to continue to launch. As I wrote earlier, while reading a book about prayer might release the spiritual tension, it is not praying. *Praying for Your Elephant* is not meant to prepare you to pray as much as it is designed to challenge you to press the button now. If you have not begun to identify your elephants and systematically pray for them in the way most meaningful to you, now is the time. As I believe most astronauts would affirm, it is better to be lost in space than to fail to launch. Push the button.

CHAPTER 5

DIGGING FOR GOLD

You can read about how to swim, but you're not
actually swimming until you get in the pool.
—Orville Stanton

THE SECRET KEY TO EFFECTIVE PRAYER

God did not intend prayer to be a magical art whose deep secrets are guarded by shrouded monks on remote islands. Nor is prayer solely a mystical experience saved for the spiritual illuminati. Rather, prayer is the common language of God's people. Prayer is the Christian's native tongue.

If prayer did have a mystical key that unlocked its treasures, it would be this—prayer. Praying is the secret key of prayer. Yes, you read that right. The key to effective, power-filled prayer is the act of praying. Taking the time to step out of your normal, frenetic existence to center yourself through prayer is the only way you will ever move forward in this journey.

In this chapter, I want to give you effective tools to create a new prayerful rhythm of life. In order for that to happen, you will need to stop orchestrating your times of conversational intimacy with God as though they are experimental jazz sessions. This means finding daily, sacred, and consistent times of prayer that are off-limits from all the good, bad, and ugly distractions competing for your time and attention. I'm challenging you to find a rhythm that works for you and to dedicate yourself to keeping that beat.

Consistency in prayer will not come and lie at your feet. You need to fight for it with a determined resolve. And this is where the foundation of prayer is laid, in resolution. People who often experience prayer in its deepest ways are people who show up most regularly, seeking God in prayer's glorious monotony.

DIGGING DEEP

I use the phrase "glorious monotony" because that is what I often experience when I go to prayer. Like a miner, I put on my hard hat and descend deep into prayer's heart. It is there that I dig, dig, dig. More often than not, I ascend from my spiritual spelunking with little perceived treasure to show for it—no emotional highs or profound spiritual experiences found. On other days, I discover a nugget of gold among the rubble, and the presence of God feels real and vibrant. And then there are those seasons when I hit the mother lode. I find a vein of God's consolation. These are the times when God pulls back the curtain for a season and prayer seems easy, spiritually fulfilling, and ultimately rewarding. In these times God's responses to my elephant prayers seem endless, consistent, and rich.

Eventually, though, those veins dry up, and I'm back in the coal mines of prayer again, choking on the black dust of difficult and monotonous prayer times. It is here that I must remind myself of the glory of monotony. Only in showing up every day, helmet on, pick in hand, and entering the vast mine that is prayer will I ever unearth any of its riches. The key to mining is digging. The key to prayer is praying.

STAKING YOUR CLAIM

If you want to mine the riches of prayer, you first need to stake your claim in the real estate of your personal time. This means surveying the territory of your life, the flow of each day's work, play, and rest, and identifying the hours, days, weeks, and seasons that you are going to claim for your own. As people of prayer, we must remember that the demands of life are a claim jumper that will infringe on your times with God if you let them.

This is something that Jesus had a keen awareness of. Time with His Father in prayer was not something He allowed to be easily stolen from Him. As was His custom, Jesus would depart from events and gatherings that most rabbis of His day would have only dreamed to be a part of for the purpose of claiming some precious time with His Father. As the gospel of Luke portrays, the more Jesus grew in popularity, the more He would withdraw for this purpose. This is something that frustrated Jesus's handlers to no end. How are you supposed to build your platform if you keep disappearing from events that grow your ministry influence? It's poor marketing strategy.

This is a lesson we can learn from Christ, especially those of us who, like Jesus, are in the "business" of professional or vocational Christianity. Jesus was much more concerned with expanding the platform of the heart than increasing His Twitter followers. The apostle Luke said, "Yet the news about him [Jesus] spread all the more, so that crowds of people came to hear him and to be healed of their sicknesses. But Jesus often withdrew to lonely places and prayed" (Luke 5:15–16). Spending time with the Father renewed Jesus for His ministry.

Christ's vigilance in protecting time with His Father was quite different from the relationship He had with His material possessions. Take money, for example. The gospel of John tells us that Jesus cared so little about being stolen from in the material realm that when it came to His personal possessions, He put Judas, a known thief to Him, in charge of His wallet. The twelfth chapter of John relates:

> Mary therefore took a pound of ointment of pure nard, very precious, and anointed the feet of Jesus, and wiped his feet with her hair: and the house was filled with the odor of the ointment.
>
> But Judas Iscariot, one of his disciples, that should betray him, saith,
>
> Why was not this ointment sold for three hundred shillings, and given to the poor?
>
> Now this he said, not because he cared for the poor; but *because he was a thief,* and having the bag took away what was put therein. (John 12:3–6 ASV)

Think about how different Jesus reacted from how we often live. If anyone were to steal even five dollars from our wallets, we would be infuriated. Call the cops! At the same time we allow some of the most meaningless and oftentimes spiritually hurtful things to rob us from times with God. Money is something that no matter how great of a sum you lose it can always be replaced. The same cannot be said for time with your Abba Father.

CUSTOMS

Today the word *habit* has taken on a negative connotation. When we think of habits, our minds tend to conjure up images of tobacco in hard red cardboard boxes, bottles filled with amber-colored liquor, and naked pictures on glossy paper and digital screens.

Customs on the other hand have a more positive understanding in modern culture. This is because customs are deeply connected to communal and personal identity. Actually, though, habits and customs aren't really that different. Both speak of consistency and repetition. You often become what you do most. Identity is rooted in custom.

The Jewish culture into which Jesus was born was steeped in customs. It was these customs that defined Hebrew identity. Because of these established customs, Israel was able to reestablish nationhood after more than two thousand years of displacement. Try doing that today with the ancient Aztecs or Babylonians. With the cessation of customs came the end of a people's connection to those civilizations. Few people today know of their origins to lost and distant civilizations. For instance, when was the last time you met someone who identified with the Mayan culture?

Jews on the other hand remained committed to their habits and customs for thousands of years after their nation was decimated, something that happened multiple times in their history. Even when Jews were dispersed, they knew who they were and where they came from. Each time after dissolution as a nation, the Hebrews were able to regroup and reclaim their identity as a people. Had the Jews not faithfully kept their traditions, they would also have lost their identity in the process. Our habits create our identity. Habitual prayer is a discipline that unleashes you into your true identity.

Jesus also was a man of habit whose identity was expressed in His customs. One of Jesus's habitual customs was prayer. He could regularly be found in the same places at the same times speaking to God. Prayer was part of Christ's identity, and in it He reaffirmed who He was and what He was called to do.

Jesus's habit of prayer was so consistent that when wanting to betray Christ, Judas did not have to ask where He was going to be that fateful night. Judas knew where He would go: the Mount of Olives. You could set your watch by Jesus's prayerful rituals. The apostle Luke said, "And he [Jesus] came out, and went, *as his custom was*, unto the Mount of Olives; and the disciples also followed him. And when he was at the place, he said unto them, Pray that ye enter not into temptation. And he was parted from them about a stone's cast; and he kneeled down and prayed" (Luke 22:39–41 ASV).

It was Jesus's custom of creating consistent, sacred space that sealed His fate. While I know these questions have no real answer in this life, sometimes I wonder what would have happened if Christ had blown off His time with His Father in the garden that night.

What would the consequences have been? Are there consequences when I give up my privileged right to go boldly before the creator of the universe and my true Father for some meaningless TV show, intriguing event, or social media distraction? I wonder.

What about you? Would the people closest to you have any idea as to your customs of prayer? I'm not suggesting that you broadcast them from the rooftops. What I am asking is, Has your custom of prayer become so habitual that those closest to you are aware of the times in your life you define as sacred space? Or are you without custom when it comes to spiritual disciplines, always doing them on the fly?

SACRED SPACE

One of the places my wife, Karie, and I have staked off as customary sacred space is a stretch of California freeway from Oceanside to San Clemente, a distance of about twenty miles. It started a half decade ago, back when we had Disneyland season passes. A couple of times a month we would pack the family in the car and make the hour-long pilgrimage to the happiest place on earth.

One of the things Karie and I looked forward to the most during those adventures had nothing to do with Mickey Mouse. After wearing the kids out for a few hours on rides and filling their bellies with sugar, we would put them in their pajamas and brush their teeth in the Pinocchio parking lot. Within a few minutes of hitting the highway toward home, the kids would be in deep sleep with visions of sugarplum fairies dancing in their heads. This was my and Karie's time to connect and settle our relationship in conversation.

After a couple of excursions, I noticed that we had randomly prayed together as a couple when driving through Camp Pendleton, a marine base that snakes along the stretch of road between Oceanside and San Clemente. I mentioned this to Karie and brought up the idea that we should dedicate this portion of road to God and make it a habitual part of our prayer life. She was easy to convince.

For the last seven years or so we have prayed as a couple or family almost every time we journey through Camp Pendleton, something we do about twice a month as my wife's parents live just past San Clemente. This habit has become an ingrained part of our family's communal life of prayer. It also has been a fertile ground of discipleship where we can model and coach our children in the gift of prayer.

This is what I mean by claiming sacred space in your life. Today if we drive through Camp Pendleton without praying, something feels wrong, out of place. We have paved this piece of spiritual highway with the concrete of our prayers.

Where are the territories in your life to which you can stake spiritual claim? Is it in your favorite chair as the sun rises or down at the lake during your lunch break? Maybe it's in your car between classes. Perhaps it's all three.

The point is this, and I say it definitively: **you need to have sacred space that is off-limits to the thieves of distraction, space where you can habitually define and remember who you are through conversational intimacy with Jesus.** This was the custom of Jesus. This is the custom of God's people. If you make it your custom, Christ will make it His and never fail to meet with you at the desired time and location you claim as yours.

THE DIFFERENCE A YEAR MAKES

Now imagine that for the next year you could have a daily appointment with any person from the past or present. Who would it be? When I consider that question, my mind immediately darts back and forth between the chronological history of this planet searching for the greatest souls and minds who have ever walked this earth. What would a year with Abraham Lincoln offer me in regard to integrity and leadership training? How would twelve months with Paul the apostle shape my theology in a way no doctorate degree ever could? What about spending a full year with King David writing worship songs or a year in the slums with Mother Teresa cleaning the wounds of the dying? Or what about another year with my dad who died long before I ever got a chance to really know him?

What we fail to understand is that when we meet with God in regular prayer and Scripture reading, we actually have the ability to gain every piece of wisdom, knowledge, and nurturing quality that all of these people possessed.

Is it not true that the totality of leadership gifts and understanding Lincoln possessed came directly from God? Was not David's heart of worship and Mother Teresa's instinctive compassion sourced from the depths of God as well? Doesn't God also have the ability to fill in all the gaps left behind in my childhood by a father who loved me but seemed to love his bottle a bit more?

The answer to all these questions is yes. However, the transfer of all this knowledge does not lie in God's desire to meet and download it into our hearts and minds, but rather it depends on our resolute intention to show up each day and meet with God. Prayer is personal discipleship by God Himself.

Eugene Peterson's *The Message* Bible addresses this tension in a frank and concise manner. His translation of Jeremiah reads this way: "If they'd have bothered to sit down and meet with me, they'd have preached my Message to my people. They'd have gotten them back on the right track, gotten them out of their evil ruts. 'Am I not a God near at hand'—GOD's Decree—'and not a God far off? Can anyone hide out in a corner where I can't see him?' GOD's Decree. 'Am I not present everywhere, whether seen or unseen?' GOD's Decree" (Jer. 23:21–24 MSG).

If that is not a two-by-four to the soul, then I don't know what is. This is the truth of just showing up. Not only will you have a concise understanding of God's message for your life, but God promises that the road of your existence will not be filled with ruts and potholes. The book of Proverbs says, "In all your ways submit to him, and he will make your paths straight" (Prov. 3:6).

Prayer is the place where we submit our ways to God. I like the way the NIV uses the word *submit* when translating the same passage rather than *acknowledge*. I think it is a word that more adequately reflects the meaning of this text. We are not to give God a tip of the cap but rather a slave's obedient submission. When we submit every area of our lives to God in prayer, He makes His ways known to us. His ways are straight and not quagmires of confusion, double mindedness, and doubt.

When prayerful submission is conjoined with dedicated and consistent time in God's Word, you create a locomotion of God's direction in your life that travels on straight and ironclad railroad tracks reaching into your future. This is much different from the twisted, bog-filled back roads that many of us have accepted as God's normal.

HEARING IT FIRSTHAND

Committing to having God be your primary form of counsel is crucial in knowing the right paths to walk on in your life. This is something I experienced recently at a pastors' conference I attended. Usually when I attend a conference, I leave feeling like a snake that needs to strip off its old skin. Everything needs to be revamped; everything is in need of change. This conference was different in that it was directly related to God's grace and a determined resolve to consistently meet with Jesus this year in prayer and Scripture reading.

While the conference was both inspiring and amazing, I left feeling like I did not need to change a thing in my own life or the ministry I lead. Instead, many things that the speakers said only confirmed what God had already shared with me. Instead of needing a gifted mediator and communicator to get me back on the right track, I already understood many of the ways in which God wanted me to walk. As a matter of fact, everything I heard at this event was filtered through the lens of my personal encounters with God in prayer and Scripture reading over the last year. This is far different from how I used to show up for events like this, desperate to have someone else tell me what God wanted me to know.

Here is a truth. Jesus did not die on a cross so that He could continue to speak to you primarily through some other person, movie, or book. Christ came and suffered to be known intimately by you and to open up the lines of communication blocked by the fall of mankind.

He came that He might speak mightily and directly to you. Scripture is clear when it says, "Let us then approach God's throne of grace with confidence, so that we may receive mercy and find grace to help us in our time of need" (Heb. 4:16). It does not say that we are to approach the throne standing behind a human mediator.

This is such a beautiful and poignant verse. The throne God sits on is a throne of grace that will offer you what you need and allow you to receive mercy and find grace. If you have been wondering where grace went in your life, you can find it at God's throne.

The kind of insider knowledge I am writing about is available to you firsthand from God. The key is committing and allowing a scripturally based and prayer-filled conversation with your heavenly Father to rule your life. This vital conversation with God mirrors many of the conversations you have every day.

CONVERSATIONAL INTIMACY

I recently heard Brian Hardin, the creator of the *Daily Audio Bible*, use the phrase "conversational intimacy with God." It seemed to hit the nail on the head and describe what we are going for when we pray. The ability to communicate clearly, perhaps passionately and with intent, is crucial. Physical touch, body language, and tone are all parts of getting your point across to others. While all of these methods are effective, none hold a candle to conversation.

In the world of communication, conversation is king. Ancient biblical literature seems much more concerned with the words that we speak and the attitude of our hearts from which they flow than many of these other types of communication. The tongue and our use of speech to communicate is a major platform of biblical teaching. The nineteenth Psalm says, "Let the words of my mouth and the meditation of my heart be acceptable in your sight, O LORD, my rock and my redeemer" (Ps. 19:14 ESV). Then in Proverbs we read, "Death and life are in the power of the tongue, and those who love it will eat its fruits" (Prov. 18:21 ESV). Our words matter.

As an author and a speaker, I use words as tools to build God's kingdom on earth. One thing I have learned along the way is that there is a major difference between being a great communicator and an exceptional conversationalist. Give me a stage and an audience and I can present ideas in ways that make sense to those listening and allow them to easily take hold of deep concepts. This gifting has not always translated into an equally powerful ability to be conversant with those around me. The art of conversation is not diatribe but rather dialogue. It is a give-and-take that thrives in an equality of speech and listening.

When the way I interact verbally with my wife drifts from dialogue to diatribe, our relationship suffers. My wife is not my audience. Her favorite topic of conversation is not me, nor is it my latest ministry project or hobby. I'm not saying that these things don't interest her, but when our conversational intimacy becomes one-sided, she often feels marginalized and the romance of conversation becomes narcissism. It's hard to love someone when you're competing with his or her love of self.

THE IMPORTANCE OF THE WORDS WE PRAY

Prayer is deeper than words, and wordless prayer has a profound place in the life of believers, but God gave us words for a reason. The

words we use in prayer matter. Not only do they communicate to God what is on our hearts, but they also help us process and refine our thoughts and feelings into tangible expression. Words are the expression of what is truly on our hearts. Jesus said, "A good man out of the good treasure of his heart brings forth good; and an evil man out of the evil treasure of his heart brings forth evil. For out of the abundance of the heart his mouth speaks" (Luke 6:45 NKJV).

God already knows what we are going to say before we say it, but when we focus on the words we choose to speak before God, we become better aware of our own selves. God gave us the gift of words for a reason; He esteems words. This is so much so that when God chose to identify Jesus in Holy Scripture, He called Him the Word. The apostle John said, "In the beginning was the Word, and the Word was with God, and the Word was God" (John 1:1).

The words you use in prayer are an important component in crafting a strategic and specific prayer life. These prayerful words are the building blocks we use in collaboration with God to create the life He has called us to, the life He wants to imagine with us into being. Prayerful words paint a vivid picture of the things you want to create on the canvas of life.

WORDS ARE CREATIVE BUILDING BLOCKS

When trying to understand the importance of words in life and kingdom creation, we again need to look no further than the beginning of time. When God expressed Himself into creation, He did so with words. God spoke the universe into creation with specific and strategic words.

> In the beginning God created the heavens and the earth. Now the earth was formless and empty, darkness was over the surface of the deep, and the Spirit of God was hovering over the waters.
>
> And God said, "Let there be light," and there was light. God saw that the light was good, and he separated the light from the darkness. God called the light "day," and the darkness he called "night." And there was evening, and there was morning—the first day. (Gen. 1:1–5)

Each time God spoke, His words were followed by action. The same can be true for our prayers. (See Dan. 9:23.) Each time we speak a prayer to God, we put it into a position to be moved on by God. Here again we are walking the tightrope I mentioned earlier. Every word we pray needs to be translated and filtered by the Holy Spirit before being presented to God, but this does not mean that we should not be aware of the words we pray. This is one of the both/ands of Scripture.

If you read through the first chapter of Genesis, you will notice one phrase repeated over and over again, "Then God said" (NASB). Ten times in this chapter alone, God speaks things into existence. God speaks strategic and specific words into nothingness, and creation rises from its void.

Here is what I find interesting. Did God need to say something every time He created? No, He did not. God could have fashioned the entire universe with a slight nod or a wink for that matter. And who was God talking to? He spoke into nothingness and from it life was formed when He spoke. When He created, He chose to use words. God demonstrated by speaking when He did not need to that words have the power to create. The words you use in prayer also matter and hold that same power when moved on by God. Prayerful words are the bricks and mortar of kingdom creation.

GOD'S WORD

Perhaps the Bible itself is God's greatest reminder to us of why the words we pray matter. Jesus was in the regular habit of incorporating Scripture into all elements of His speech. He used Scripture when He debated with the Pharisees and the Devil. He spoke Scripture as a discipleship tool in the training of the disciples and to fulfill prophecy when hanging on the cross. A knowledge and use of Scripture was deeply integrated into His prayer life. Jesus understood that Scripture is where the power is.

One of the most powerful tools you can use in prayer is also infusing God's Word into your personal prayers. I want to challenge you to begin creating a book of prayers, prayers you have written and that come from your heart. You, like David, can create and record your own personal prayers and petitions built on the powerful promises of Scripture. Perhaps these prayers will even become a spiritual legacy as they are passed down from generation to generation.

As you go about creating your own personal book of psalms, you will want to blend in a high volume of biblical content. King David excelled at this. David was a wordsmith, a master craftsman who deeply understood God's law. As you read through the Psalms, you see David's unique ability to blend the situations of his life and

God's law. When you emulate King David in personal psalm or prayer creation, your very life will become entwined and knotted together with God's Word. The prayers you create will be a powerful kingdom-building tool that God promises will never come back without fulfilling their purposes. (See Isa. 55:11.)

BUILDING YOUR PRAYER LIFE ONE SENTENCE AT A TIME

So how do we do this? It's really not that hard, but like most things in your prayer life, it will not be done without determined resolve. The crafting of these specific and strategic sentences is crucial to the message of the elephant and something I have found incredibly effective in changing my life.

Last year when my wife lost her brother to suicide, a deep, sorrowful pall settled over our family. As you can imagine, it was and still is a season of emotional ups and downs. Grief is like a knotted ball of yarn. It is not something that can be cut through with scissors but must rather be painstakingly unknotted. After Devin's death I immediately crafted strategic, Scripture-laden prayers to guide us through this time. Two of the verses that I chose to embed into my prayers were the following:

> Sarah said, "God has made laughter for me; everyone who hears will laugh with me." (Gen. 21:6 NASB)

> Strength and dignity are her clothing, and she smiles at the future. (Prov. 31:25 NASB)

Here is how I have steeped my prayers for my wife and family in these verses. These are actual prayers I pray from my personal journal.

- Dear God, would You *make laughter* for Karie? I pray that on our family nights she would experience deep joy and laughter as You heal her from this pain. May she *laugh with us*.
- Dear Jesus, allow Karie to redeem the past as she mourns the loss of her brother and *smile as she looks toward the future*.

Do you see how I embedded the words of Scripture into my own self-created prayers? These two prayers have yielded so much fruit-filled healing in our lives it would be hard to put it into words. What I can say is that while Karie has grieved, she has not been incapacitated with depression, something she has struggled with all her life.

There have also been numerous times during our intentional family Tuesday nights, the name for our family nights, when Karie has laughed so hard it has almost made her cry. This is the power that Scripture has to change your life when grafted into your prayer time. I'm not sure what our lives would look like had I not prayed these prayers. All I know is that I did and God moved. He can do the same for you.

LIFE VERSES

Think about the verses that have changed your life. Imagine if you began to let those verses invade your prayer life. Like a rudder plunged deep into the waters of your life, those verses will guide your course in the direction of their intent.

This understanding is new for me and has drastically reframed my prayer life. Today I spend as much time crafting the scriptural words I use in prayer as I do praying those sentences into existence.

Before I started this practice, I would sit in prayer and say whatever emerged. While I still observe this in an effort to allow the Spirit to lead the conversation, the majority of my prayer life is not created from a platform of random thoughts but rather from the anchor of God's Word.

Today I highly value the precise and exact sentences, requests, and petitions I have disciplined myself to create in collaboration with God. Instead of throwing out prayer like darts without a board, now I have a target. By sitting with God in asking prayer, He has given me a vision and helped me define exactly what I want to see built in my life. This practice has brought a real purpose and passion to my times of conversational intimacy with God. Now my encounters with God in prayer are not defined by the random, unfinished sentences of the past but rather are Scripture filled and purposeful.

PRAYING SCREWTAPE'S WAY

In *The Screwtape Letters* written by C. S. Lewis, Screwtape says to Wormwood in speaking about prayer, "He may be persuaded to aim at something entirely spontaneous, inward, informal, and unregularised."[1]

While some of you might balk at the suggestion that we need to structure our prayer times to the point of crafting the actual verse-filled sentences we pray, Screwtape, the senior demon mentoring a junior demon on the art of spiritual attack, encourages the type of prayer that is without habit, without custom, and without intentional specificity.

What Lewis emphasized in *The Screwtape Letters* is that prayerful targets matter. Unstructured prayer times have their place, but when they make up the lion's share of your time with God, you have a potential problem.

Why do we tend to believe this when it comes to the physical things we do in life but not the spiritual? Can you grow a diverse and productive garden without hard work and care? Can you build a three-story home without plans? Can you drive to a place you have never been to without a road map? But this is exactly what we do with our prayers.

NO SECRETS

While I have tried my best to give you some tools for the journey in this chapter, the truth remains that there are no real secrets to prayer other than praying. Yes, these possible solutions might be powerful releasers of God's intention for you and your prayers, but whether you choose to use them or some other form of prayer is really up to you. The key is prayer, and if you choose to use this key, it will unlock an eternity of God's wildest blessings. May you dive deep in the ocean of God's response as you call on His name.

UNDERSTANDING ELEPHANTS

Hey Adam,

As you know, I lost my job last year. In October, I decided to apply for unemployment for the first time in my life. After three months and still no movement with the unemployment board, I was frustrated. I had been living off of savings but I didn't know how much longer I could do that without a financial strain.

After you spoke a couple of weeks ago on "breakthroughs," I emailed a group of women in our group and asked them to pray very specifically for a breakthrough and for the release of the funds to me by the end of January.

About a week later, my roommate Jenn was talking with someone she knows who mentioned contacting my assemblyman. I decided maybe this was the way God was answering my prayer so the next morning I contacted my assemblyman's office and they got back to me the same day.

On Saturday the 27th of January, they called me! After asking me a few questions, they finalized my paperwork (or whatever they needed to *do; they never explained why there had been a delay) and said I would get my debit card that week. I had been praying that this would get resolved by the end of January because I was starting to wonder how I was going to pay rent, etc. The card came in the mail on Saturday, February 1, with back pay for the four months prior.*

To me this was a real answer to prayer! In it I was never worried, thankfully, but felt confident that God would provide, but this was a clear indication to me that God used these ladies to move a mountain in His kingdom. Thanks for encouraging us to pray more and to pray for one another. I truly believe I would still be waiting for these funds if we had not prayed!

Thanks for leading the migration!

Jen

CHAPTER 6

OOMPA-LOOMPAS

Daddy, I want an Oompa-Loompa! I want you to
get me an Oompa-Loompa right away!
—Veruca Salt in *Willy Wonka and the Chocolate Factory*

I WANT AN OOMPA-LOOMPA RIGHT AWAY!

Remember Veruca Salt? In the famous children's novel by Roald Dahl, *Charlie and the Chocolate Factory*, Veruca was the petulant daughter of a placating father who made it his mission in life to grant her every wish. Her big solo number in the movie *Willy Wonka and the Chocolate Factory* sums up her view on life. She vows to scream if she doesn't get the whole world, and she doesn't care how she gets it. She wants it all now!

Eventually, Veruca's desire to have whatever she wants at any cost leads to her demise as she descends deep into the bowels of Willy's factory and is eventually deposited in the rubbish bin. **Sometimes the worst thing that can happen in your life is to get what you want, to get whatever your heart desires.**

The tendency to oversalt our prayers with too much of our own desires is something most of us struggle with. Prayer is not an altar built unto self. At the same time there are plenty of verses in the Holy Scriptures that point to the fact that God delights in bringing our personal desires to fruition. Psalm 20:4 speaks about God bringing you the desires of your heart while causing your plans to succeed. Psalm 37 declares, "Take delight in the LORD, and he will give you the desires of your heart" (Ps. 37:4). So what's the answer? How are we to find the middle ground between selfishness and bold asking?

Here again, the art of wise balance is essential. Think of a tight-rope over Niagara Falls. Yes, we need to steer clear of those extreme brands of Christianity that have built entire doctrines on the principle of naming something in the moniker of Jesus and then claiming it as our own in faith. At the same time, we must be equally careful not to allow guilt to shepherd our prayers into dry and confined pastures. Extravagant asking in Jesus's name is part of a well-balanced prayer life.

Here's the difference between the two. Many gospel messages that promise prosperity are an if/then proposition. They say if you do this or that in a certain manner or employ a precise formula of God manipulation, God will then in turn be obligated to fulfill His end of the bargain or promise and bless you beyond your wildest dreams.

We see this in the various brands of Christian faith that rather than emphasize the cross of Christ use healing or generosity as their primary platforms. The thought is that God is so desperate to bless you, to heal you, that if you can give that extra penny more or believe a little more purely in the name of faith, God will be given the green light to open the floodgates of heaven. This if/then spirituality seems closer to witchcraft than biblical Christianity to me. Prayer is not the casting of spells. Witchcraft is based in control. Prayer is rooted in submission.

While it is true that God is not a liar and will do what He says He will do, we must not be arrogant enough to believe that the way He fulfills His promises will match the way we think He will respond to them. Nor should we be foolish enough to believe that the claims Jesus makes about answering prayer are devoid of construct. The bold claim to answer whatever we ask for in Jesus's name is snugly nestled between right relationship with God, proper motive, and His divine will.

Bold asking prayer is not an incantation that forces God's hand just because you use His name in the invoking of that request. The movement of God on our prayers is always a mixture of grace and God's will, not a concoction of two bat wings and the eye of newt. The prosperity gospel misuses the verse that says, "God is not man, one given to lies, and not a son of man changing his mind. Does he speak and not do what he says? Does he promise and not come through?" (Num. 23:19 MSG).

We need to pursue things like generosity, believing faith for healing, and asking prayer in our lives because Jesus pursued them in His life. We chase after these things not because of what we can get but because they are things Jesus Himself has commanded us to do for very specific reasons. (See John 15:7, 16.)

When we give, we do so not demanding or expecting any-thing from God in return. Christians should not be like credit card companies that lavishly give but expect steep repayment rates. Jesus gave His whole life away and received a cross in return. The reward He received did not come in this life. (See Phil. 2:5–11.) As a matter of fact, the reward He received was something He once possessed. He gave away that which He would reinherit. When we give or pray, we want to do so without the expectation of a return on our investment but rather with hope in Jesus. (See Rom. 12:12.)

Here again we stand on the razor blade of deep, believing faith and loose expectations.

Recently I received an email from a man going through a divorce with his wife. He entered the courtroom with deep and prayerful faith that God would have the judge rule in his favor. He left the courtroom dejected and angry at God, who in his words "had not covered or protected him through it." While I empathize with my friend and want to be there standing in the gap with him, he entered the courtroom believing that God would do a certain thing in a certain way because he had prayed. When that did not happen, God was on the hook for his disappointment. Sometimes God answers our prayers with a cross rather than the response we so desire. This is a hard truth, but truth nonetheless.

This is a reality that is rarely preached from pulpits of prosperity, because it's hard to market the cross unless you're selling gold- and diamond-encrusted ones to hang around people's necks. Faith is believing in the "He can" of God, not the "He will" of God. If you don't lodge this firmly in your personal theology, you may be putting your walk of faith in great jeopardy. The Devil preys on those who feel God has let them down when they believed with all their hearts. Perceived unanswered prayer has caused many to shipwreck their faith on the rocks of disappointment.

THE AUDACITY OF JESUS

Still, the audacity of Jesus in the fifteenth chapter of John, commanding us not once but twice to ask anything in His name, needs to be taken seriously. Jesus said,

> If you abide in Me, and My words abide in you, ask *whatever* you wish, and it will be done for you. My Father is glorified by this, that you bear much fruit, and so prove to be My disciples....
>
> You did not choose Me but I chose you, and appointed you that you would go and bear fruit, and that your fruit would remain, so that *whatever* you ask of the Father in My name He may give to you. This I command you, that you love one another. (John 15:7–8, 16–17 NASB)

Christ's redundancy in these verses was for a distinct purpose. The Son of God need not repeat Himself. Perhaps He was concerned we would miss the point: relationship, not answers, is what's important. We established this concept in chapter 1. Jesus knows that asking prayer puts us smack-dab in the middle of familial relationship with God. Jesus is giving us the thing we need in the guise of what we might want. Jesus knows our need is far superior to what we might want.

MORE THAN CHOCOLATE

Think back to Willy Wonka. Wonka offered mouthwatering chocolate bars wrapped in shiny golden tickets. Why Wonka did this was not for the reasons those who sought these golden-wrapped bars imagined. No one understood Wonka's endgame. The lucky five who found the golden tickets had only hoped for a chance to go behind the walls of the factory, meet Wonka, eat his secret treats, and receive a lifetime supply of chocolate. What more could anyone want? We are so easily satisfied.

What none of those fortunate few could have imagined was that Wonka wanted to give away more than just chocolate; he wanted to give away his entire legacy. He was searching for someone to mentor, someone to have deep relationship with, someone to share the deepest of secrets with, someone to take over the entire operation.

While Jesus wants to partner with you in bringing to life your heart's desires, He also wants to give you more than just chocolate. He wants to give you eternity in the person of Himself. Jesus encourages asking prayer because in the rough-and-tumble of God's responses, we come to know our Father. We come to know Jesus.

As I wrote in the first chapter, prayer is about relationship, not answers. Answers happen on the way to relationship. Answers build relationship. The more you ask for, the more you will know Him. This is why Jesus so deeply desires to partner with us in creative, game-changing prayer. When Jesus says "Ask anything," what He is really saying is "Come to know Me through the adventure of asking prayer."

And we must take Jesus at His word. We must be willing to ask. We must be willing to shun disappointment in the hope that God might move. God is longing to respond to your prayers. He delights in them. God created prayer for the sake of relationships. The answers are just icing on the cake.

VOLUMINOUS ASKING

The art of voluminous asking is something we can learn from Veruca Salt. Veruca asked for every single thing she wanted. There are few places, if any, in God's Word that forbid abundant asking prayer when done in right relationship. Yes, there are some scriptures that point to asking with wrong motivations (see James 4:2–3), but none that govern the amount you can ask for when done in right relationship.

Where Veruca failed was not in the asking, but in her attitude. Veruca cared about precious little other than herself. I am assuming this is not true of you. And if it's not, then you are free to open up the floodgates of asking. We serve a God who dwells in eternity. Is it actually possible to ask too much when God has no measure and no shortage of resources? If there is lack, I can assure you that it comes not from God but instead from our shortfall of determination in asking prayer.

THE GRAND CANYON'S PARKING LOT AND THE THREEFOLD MISSION OF ASKING PRAYER

As with the majority of Scripture, the depth and beauty of John 15 will not be found at first glance. If we shrink and confine this teaching of Christ down to a diatribe on God's desire to grant all of your wishes, dreams, and desires, we miss out on God's mission for this passage. It would be like pulling into the parking lot of the Grand Canyon, never getting out of your car, and then returning home with stories of your amazing trip to see Arizona's greatest treasure. If you are going to really experience the Grand Canyon in all of its grandeur, not only do you need to get out of your vehicle, but you need to stand on its rim, perhaps even descend into its heart.

Let's revisit and expound on the threefold kingdom-building mission of asking prayer that I introduced in chapter 1. Again, the mission of asking prayer is to glorify God, that those who pray would bear much fruit, and that answered prayer would be a proof of discipleship.

In the simplicity of one sentence, Jesus took asking prayer from a one-dimensional "ask and receive" proposition to a multifaceted kingdom-building mission where God is glorified, your life and ministry are propagated in abundance, and evangelism happens. Jesus said, "If you abide in Me, and My words abide in you, ask *whatever* you wish, and it will be done for you. My Father is glorified by this, that you bear much fruit, and so prove to be My disciples" (John 15:7–8 NASB).

This is perhaps the most crucial truth of this entire book. **Asking prayer is not solely about us or the elephants we desire.** When we ask in prayer, we are becoming kingdom builders. If you want to build God's kingdom on earth, then you need to become committed to voluminous asking prayer.

GLORIFYING THE FATHER

Make no mistake about it. Jesus came to earth for one specific purpose—to glorify the Father. For God so loved the world that He sent His only Son that we might be saved from destruction, but saving humanity was not Christ's primary purpose. Jesus's primary purpose was to glorify God. Everything else Jesus did by coming to earth was ancillary to that goal. Here are just a couple of scriptural references to that end. The book of John says, "Jesus spoke these things, looked up to heaven, and said: Father, the hour has come. Glorify Your Son so that the Son may glorify You" (John 17:1 HCSB). Earlier in the book of John, Jesus said, "'Father, glorify Your name!' Then a voice came from heaven: 'I have glorified it, and I will glorify it again!'" (John 12:28 HCSB).

Few of us like arrogant people. Nothing is more boring than people who talk only about themselves. If we look at God's commitment to continually bring attention to His own glory with human understanding, it is easy to stumble. Questions jump into our minds about a God who is so insecure that He constantly needs to bring glory to Himself.

When we step back and see through a biblical lens, we realize that everything God does is deserving of glory. When God glorifies Himself, He is acting in truth. This is not true for man, and we must not apply our feeble understanding of what is right or wrong for mankind to what is right or wrong for God. When a man glorifies himself, he is acting in error, for all that he has to exalt in himself was given to him by God. Man never has a right for self-exaltation. Not so for God. For God not to have His glory as the final destination for all His works and actions would be to deny the truth. For God to walk in truth, the end of all His actions must point to His glory. This includes coming to earth to save mankind.

An example of God's glory being the summation of each thing He does would be creation itself. God made creation, and the

Scriptures tell us that creation itself exclaims His glory. While creation has many functions, its ultimate product is God's glory: "The heavens declare the glory of God, and the sky above proclaims his handiwork" (Ps. 19:1 ESV).

When Jesus commanded His people to ask for anything in His name, He did it knowing that His Father would be glorified in the process. God answers your prayers because it glorifies Him. Again, this is not arrogant of God; it is God living in the truth of Himself. God is being God.

Asking prayer is one of the best ways for you to bring glory to God. The more you ask for, the more opportunities you will have to see God glorified. This is true for the prayers in your life that seem of utmost importance and those that seem insignificant. This is true for the prayers to which God says yes and the ones to which He says no.

STARBUCKS, A LEATHER CHAIR, AND GOD'S GLORY

A few years back, I was sitting in Starbucks and noticed they had just gotten some new leather chairs. I asked the barista where I could get one. He told me they were specifically made for Starbucks and not available to the public.

Not wanting to accept no for an answer, which is often the case with me, I went over to the chair and looked for a label that could identify its maker. To my consternation, all the labels had been removed. Frustrated, I turned to the web. I would ferret out the information one way or another. To my surprise, no matter how hard I searched, I could not find anything online that pointed to the chair's maker. A conspiracy was obviously afoot. With nowhere left to turn, I offered up a little prayer to God asking if He could somehow hook me up with one of those chairs. Before I left the store that day, I had forgotten about that prayer. I never prayed it again.

Fast-forward a few years as I'm vacuuming my living room. While our living room is well appointed, it had one glaring deficiency—a leather chair. Granted, my world was not going to end if I did not get one, but the thought of having a really nice place to sit and read each night was quite alluring. Those of you who are bookish understand.

Since committing to asking prayer as a lifestyle, I've learned the lesson of praying for something and waiting before I go out and buy it in my own power. Yes, we had the cash on hand to buy the chair I wanted, but why do anything in my flesh if God might have a better and more adventurous plan? So I prayed for a chair as I vacuumed the carpet. At the exact moment my random prayer for a leather chair ended, a thought popped into my mind: *check Craigslist for a leather chair.* Was this thought from God? I didn't know, but there seemed no harm in assuming it might be, so I decided to give it a try. I stopped vacuuming, opened my computer, and began searching. Right there at the top of the page was an amazing leather chair priced at twenty-five dollars. Skeptical, I called the seller, who said she had gotten a call from another potential buyer who might come after work, but if I could get there earlier, I could have it. I jumped in my ugly yellow truck and rushed over.

Within thirty minutes I had one of the most beautiful leather chairs I could want in the bed of my truck. Here's the crazy part. As

I unloaded it, the seat cushion fell out and exposed its underbelly. There in large letters and on a tag that had not been removed were the words "Made exclusively for Starbucks." Immediately, the prayer I had prayed a few years earlier came back to my mind. I was blown away. Not only had God provided me an awesome leather chair, but He had remembered a prayer I long ago had forgotten. I love the adventure of prayer! So what does that have to do with God's glory? I'll tell you. A few days after I bought the chair, a friend of mine was at my home and commented on what a beautiful leather chair I had. When I told him the story, he said, "Wow, isn't God rad!" I got a chair, and God got the glory. That's how it works. This is true whether you are praying for leather chairs or starting orphanages in Cambodia. Hopefully, you pray for both and see God glorified in each. Praying for leather chairs and the plight of orphans need not be mutually exclusive.

BEARING MUCH FRUIT

If you are a Christian, you will bear fruit. If you are encapsulated in Christ's love with the indwelling presence and power of the Holy Spirit, you will have some level of crop production.

The difference between whether you produce an abundant harvest or only a few pieces of tiny and emaciated fruit is prayer. Jesus, in the book of John, assumed fruit production for those who abide in Christ. The difference between the amount you harvest is prayer. Prayer takes you into the "much-ness" of God.

Whenever we deal with portions of Scripture that point to mankind's ability to manipulate outcomes through our own choices, we sink into murky theological territory. Does prayer really change things that God would not have done anyway? Can choosing not to pray hinder God, or will He have His way whether or not we pray?

These tail-chasing conversations are great for deepening thought and understanding of God's Word and work in the world, but they are also effective at causing spiritual paralysis. This is definitely true when it comes to asking prayer. I know many believers who end up not praying because of doubt in prayer's ability to change things or a deep belief in God's complete sovereignty in all situations. **Theology should be the fuel of action, but so often it is the poison of inaction.** Whether the prayerful chicken came before or after the egg really doesn't matter to me. The key is that Jesus commanded us to pray for both in bold asking prayer. No matter where you stand on the issues of God's governance, it should not matter when it comes to how much you pray. Pray as much as you can. Pray as much as you are willing. In the first letter to the Thessalonians, Paul said, "Rejoice always; pray without ceasing; in everything give thanks; for this is God's will for you in Christ Jesus" (1 Thess. 5:16–18 NASB).

When Jesus talks about maximizing the crop production of our lives, He is speaking about more than putting a few more dollars in our wallets or persuading people to attend our churches. Don't get me wrong, I think Jesus means that also, but we must remember that Jesus views all things through an eternal perspective.

Jesus understands that when we pray we enshroud the things we pray for with eternity. This happens because prayer is the eternal language of God. Anything that ends up being spoken in eternity becomes eternal. I wrote about this in chapter 1, and it is something that the apostle John witnessed firsthand during his revelations on the isle of Patmos. John said, "And when he had taken it, the four living creatures and the twenty-four elders fell down before the Lamb. Each one had a harp and they were holding golden bowls full of incense, which are the prayers of God's people" (Rev. 5:8).

This verse exclaims a radical truth. You have the ability to mark eternity each time you pray. Like a tattoo in heaven, the things you pray for immediately become not only a fixture but also the fragrance of heaven, burning as incense before God. When we get to heaven, its distinctive smell will be that rendered from the burning poultice of thousands of years of prayer. Every time you pray, your prayers become part of the contents of this smoking bowl mentioned in John's Revelation. There your prayers will burn forever with the prayers of Paul the apostle, Mother Teresa, and the believing plumber who lives down the street from you.

So what does this have to do with fruit production? When we pray, we are living in the eternal now by thrusting the hope of our lives and world into forever in the form of prayer. The thing to remember is that prayer is not a one-way trip. Rather, prayer reverberates back and forth between God's throne and this world. God does not let prayer sit before Him with inaction. Rather, He responds to prayer. In the same way our prayers mark eternity, eternity marks our lives and world when God touches our petitions through response. This interplay between heaven and earth is one element of the manifested kingdom of God on earth and is displayed in the book of Matthew. Jesus said, "This, then, is how you should pray: 'Our Father in heaven, hallowed be your name,

your kingdom come, your will be done, on earth as it is in heaven'"
(Matt. 6:9–10).

The Father's response to our prayers brings and builds God's
kingdom on earth. It also guarantees that we are not laboring in
vain. This is the first and primary way that God brings His much-
ness into our lives. The things you pray for immediately transition
to a position of eternality from one that was previously mired in
the temporal. The much-ness of eternity has increased your limited
existence now just by being connected to it in asking prayer.

One of the qualities of eternity is that it is abundant. I don't
believe it is possible to have eternity touch today without that
abundance affecting and increasing the now of our existence. I have
experienced this so many times. I will pray for something, perhaps
the ability to take my family on a vacation or for volunteers to help
in a ministry project, and be overwhelmed with response from God
so far beyond what I had prayed for. I end up with the ability to
bless others. Here again we ride the tailwind of prayer.

This happened recently when I prayed for God to supply volunteers for a ministry event. So many people volunteered that I was
able to offer some to other ministries also needing help that day.

The simple point is this: When we pray, we entrust God with
the results of our now. God, who lives in abundance, gets to the
business of doing things His way and with His resources. These
unlimited resources far exceed anything we could ever do or hope
for in our power. The result of God's intervention is the bearing of
fruit in line with the much-ness of God.

In the end it is your choice. Bear only the fruit that comes
inherently with being a child of God, or bear an abundance of fruit

that comes with committing the things of this life and your world to God in asking prayer.

PROOF THAT YOU ARE HIS DISCIPLE

Every week on Tuesday afternoons I meet my friend Jamie down at the beach to take a run along the coast. I met Jamie at a wedding at which I officiated, and we hit it off right away. Jamie is a forty-something man who owns a string of successful restaurants here in San Diego. Fast as a gazelle and wise as an owl, Jamie has become a good friend. Ironically, I officiated at Jamie's wedding last year. He was raised in a family that considered themselves Christians, but by his own admission, he has never taken the jump to completely following Jesus.

In the last three years, Jamie and I have run hundreds of miles together. When we started running, I was careful about what I spoke to him. I was told by a mutual friend that he was skeptical about religion, and when the topic came up, he would avoid it like the plague.

As the months passed and the miles unfolded before us, so did our relationship. Few places yield themselves to authentic conversation like the open road. As our trust began to grow, we shared our lives in deeper, more meaningful ways. Conversations about football and food transitioned to those about values and eternity. Questions were asked in each direction, and answers were found.

As we ran, I would often share what I was currently praying about. When I started sharing these things with Jamie, I had no agenda other than to be authentic. What I did not expect was how powerful of an evangelistic witness these prayers would become.

This is because Jamie began to witness God answering my prayers. I would tell Jamie something I was petitioning God about, and during the next week or month I would come back with a radical story about how God had moved. On a few occasions, God answered random prayers Jamie was aware of during our runs.

Before long, Jamie asked if I would pray for things in his life. Finding a wife and starting a family were on the top of his priority list. As I prayed, Jamie began to experience answered prayer too. It blew his mind. Sometime last year at the end of one of our runs, he asked if I would pray over something for him. I asked if he would mind me praying right there on the street corner. He was game, and so I prayed right there in broad daylight. Today we end many of our runs in prayer even though Jamie has still not made a commitment to Christ.

The cool part of the story is this. The last time we ran, Jamie asked me about what kind of Bible he should buy. He wanted to start reading Scripture and look into what it means to follow Christ. This is what Jesus meant when He said that asking prayer proves that you are His disciple.

The icing on the cake of this story is that last year, Jamie asked me to officiate at his wedding. Today when we meet for our runs, the stories we share have changed. This is because Jamie is also the proud new parent of a baby boy. Elephants!

A MOST EFFECTIVE FORM OF EVANGELISM

Asking prayer is perhaps one of the most effective evangelism tools of the modern age. We live in a culture that has a diminishing interest in Jesus and the church. While the gospel is God's power for the salvation of mankind (see Rom. 1:16), the way in which we share it might need to change. I have found that very few people today accept Christ because of well-positioned arguments or powerful testimonies. Hearts have grown cold. (See Matt. 24:12.)

What I have found, though, is that people are still interested in prayer. They might not know to whom they should pray, but if you offer to pray for them, they generally say yes. I have never had a person I offered to pray for say no. I have asked to pray for hundreds of people, many of whom are not followers of Jesus.

This is something I highly encourage you to implement into the daily rhythm of your life. It's very simple to do.

The next time someone tells you how she is doing and mentions something worthy of prayer, such as a sick child or a lost job, ask if she would mind if you pray for her. I'm not suggesting you pray for her there in that moment, at least not yet, but let her know that you will pray for her during your private prayer times. The next step is pretty simple. Go home and pray. Add her request to your specific and strategic prayer list, perhaps finding a scripture that you can incorporate into that prayer. The next time you see her, ask how her situation is going. If God has responded to your prayer for her, encourage her and tell her you will keep praying. Before long you might be surprised that she is asking you to pray for other things in her life. In this way, you have given margin in this relationship to allow God to prove that you are His disciple. When the world knows that you are His disciple, there is a good chance they might want to become followers also. This is the evangelistic mission of asking prayer.

A VISION

In this chapter I have tried to give you the scriptural vision for asking prayer that is beyond yourself. If you commit to consistent, bold, and strategic asking prayer, God will expand the boundaries of your life. Not only will the glory of God radiate into the normalcy of your daily existence, but you will begin to experience the abundance that comes with entrusting your desires, hopes, and dreams to God in prayer. Finally, and if you are bold enough to step out, you will begin to solidify your witness to the world that you are a follower of Christ. Again, all you have to do is ask.

CHAPTER 7

YOU CAN DO NOTHING

There is no way that Christians in a private capacity can do so much to promote the work of God, and advance the kingdom of Christ, as by prayer.
—Jonathan Edwards

Imagine a major publishing company contacting you about writing the story of your life. Excited, you sit down and bang out three hundred of the most fascinating pages ever put to paper. Your story is filled with great heroic accounts, fascinating tales from all over the world, and a love story Hollywood would fawn over.

Now imagine turning that story over to the editor. In the editor's hand is a giant eraser. As the editor reads through the account of your life, he begins erasing what he sees. The more he reads, the more he erases.

When you finally receive the edited manuscript, you find that your one-hundred-thousand-word masterpiece has been trimmed down to a paltry 11,624 words. At the bottom of the final page is a note rescinding the deal that says, "We're sorry to inform you that there is not enough here of substance to work with."

This is a true story. God, the author and perfecter of your faith, has offered you a deal to publish the events of your life into heaven's eternity. The only stipulation is that the only stories that will be accepted are those that were coauthored with Him. The book of Hebrews talks about God's authorship: "Fixing our eyes on Jesus, the author and perfecter of faith, who for the joy set before Him endured the cross, despising the shame, and has sat down at the right hand of the throne of God" (Heb. 12:2 NASB).

Like a publishing deal with God, each day you are writing the words, pages, and chapters that will make up the final account of your existence here on earth. The phrases and stories that you coauthored with God will be kept for final publication in His eternity, but the bits you wrote on your own will be scrapped on the editing room floor.

Prayer in alignment with God's desires sets the ink of our lives for eternity. When we write stories for ourselves separate from Jesus—separate from prayer—those stories, like vanishing ink, dissolve from the pages of our eternal narrative. When you do ministry in your own power, it turns to dust. The business you run, if not run in alignment with God's intention, will pass away with no eternal impact. The amazing marriage and family life you have will be a forgotten tale if not typeset in God's true story.

We want to write stories that will be remembered in heaven, stories that glorify God and speak to our true identity. When we don't, our meaningless stories, no matter how impressive in this natural order, will pass away like the memory of our previous sins and sufferings. The book of Revelation confirms the passing away of things not in alignment with God's authorship when it says, "He will wipe every tear from their eyes. There will be no more death or mourning or crying or pain, for the old order of things has passed away" (Rev. 21:4).

The Old Testament speaks to the vanity of doing things in our own power this way: "Unless the LORD builds the house, those who build it labor in vain. Unless the LORD watches over the city, the watchman stays awake in vain" (Ps. 127:1 ESV).

Jesus is not only that prize-winning author spoken about in Hebrews, He is also the merciless editor who accepts no unneeded sentences, words, or ideas that water down the story. And this is crucial to understanding how and why God answers prayer. When we pray for stories in our lives that are not in step with the eternal purposes of God, they get edited out. The opposite is true for the story lines of our lives that are created through prayer and in step with God's will. These go on to glory, making the final cut. Understanding which story lines to pray over and follow happens through abiding in Christ.

FRUITLESS GARDENS AND ABIDING IN CHRIST

If you remember from the last chapter, I wrote that one of the threefold purposes of asking prayer is to maximize fruit production in our lives. The book of John makes this fully clear, this time using the imagery of Christ as the great gardener of our lives. Here, John highlights the balance between lives that yield a massive harvest and those with a poverty of production. Jesus said:

I am the true vine, and my Father is the vine-
dresser. Every branch in me that does not bear
fruit he takes away, and every branch that does
bear fruit he prunes, that it may bear more fruit.
Already you are clean because of the word that I
have spoken to you. Abide in me, and I in you.
As the branch cannot bear fruit by itself, unless
it abides in the vine, neither can you, unless you
abide in me. I am the vine; you are the branches.
Whoever abides in me and I in him, he it is that
bears much fruit, for apart from me *you can do
nothing*. If anyone does not abide in me he is
thrown away like a branch and withers; and the
branches are gathered, thrown into the fire, and
burned. (John 15:1–6 ESV)

The book of John starts this passage in the negative, showing
Christ pruning out what is not necessary before highlighting the
fruit production that comes with abiding in Him.

I want you to get in touch with this concept of nothingness.
Nothing is a big word. *Nothing* is infinity in reverse. We tend to see
nothing as that state that existed before God touched it in the work
of creation. But this cannot be further from the truth. Nothing had
no existence. When God came to the canvas of creation, even nothing failed to exist. If nothing had existed before the creation, then
it means that nothing had a substance He could work with. It did
not. Instead, God came to an absolute and utter void. Like eternity,
nothingness is something beyond the human mind to comprehend.

Nothing is what the events of your life will amount to in the end if not created, coauthored, and grown through Christ.

The book of John shows how God breathes life into nothingness: "In the beginning was the Word, and the Word was with God, and the Word was God. He was with God in the beginning. All things were created through Him, and apart from Him not one thing was created that has been created" (John 1:1–3 HCSB).

When we pray, we submit our nothingness to Jesus. As He did at the beginning of time, Christ then breathes life into that abyss. Prayer then becomes a powerful tool through which Christ creates our lives in partnership with us. It's really your choice: you have the extraordinary tool of abiding prayer to create an eternally impactful life, or you can choose to live in your nothingness. Prayer keeps our lives from meaning nothing in the end. A life of infinite meaning is what is created when we abide in Christ.

ABIDING BRANCHES

Before you throw your hands up in surrender, thinking that you probably don't meet the abiding requirements of Jesus when it comes to seeing your prayers answered, I want you to hear this. Jesus loves you. Jesus loves you now. Jesus is not waiting to love the self-created, cleaned-up, and perfect future version of you.

Yes, Christ is a merciless editor and pruner of our lives and stories, but this meticulous work of life creation through prayer is separate from how He feels about you. When you come to Him in prayer and petition, it is much more like a child coming to hug her loving father than approaching a hard-driving taskmaster with clenched fist and braided whip. Jesus is not looking for perfection in relationship. Jesus is looking *for* relationship. He already took care of the perfection bit.

The asking prayer that Jesus entreats us to pray in His name is offered to us with an understanding that we will pray it within the confines of a deeply connected and intimate relationship with God's will and ways. What you must understand is that as a redeemed child of God, you are by nature already in that position. For you to change that position, you will have to work really hard. You will have to become calloused and hardened to God. You will have to deny Christ completely. Many people of faith would say this is something that is impossible for someone who has truly come to know Christ in the first place, as nothing can separate us from the love of God. The apostle Paul said, "And I am convinced that nothing can ever separate us from God's love. Neither death nor life, neither angels nor demons, neither our fears for today nor our worries about tomorrow—not even the powers of hell can separate us from God's love" (Rom. 8:38 NLT).

Here again we are confronted with the word *nothing*. This time Scripture is not talking about nothing being created apart from Jesus, but rather that nothing can separate you from the love of God. Once more we are walking the tightrope of God's message. The Word of God says that if you are separate from God you can do nothing, but it also says that nothing can separate you from His love once you are within the confines of it.

The balance is found in understanding that nothing can change the way God feels about us in Christ but that He also won't bless what we try to do outside of His intention. This is for our own good, as it is impossible for a perfect Father to bless something that is not good for us.

This is something we must implant deep into our theological understanding. It is possible to be fully within the confines of an abiding relationship while at the same time making mistakes and decisions that are outside of His will. If this were not true, it would mean that we would have to maintain spiritual perfection to see God answer our prayers. Our life in Christ does not mirror a game of playground hopscotch where we jump in and out of favor with God like squares on a blacktop.

Instead, the connective relationship with God that is spoken of in Scripture is an eternal commodity and not based on the daily ebb and flow of our successes and failures of the spiritual life. Yes, we can create blockages in the outworking of that relationship by not abiding within His will and Word, but we are not severed from the branch of abiding because of a failure to maintain spiritual perfection or by making a mistake in our understanding of what God is calling us to do.

FEELING LIKE A FAILURE

Feeling like a failure before God is a major stumbling block for many believers when dealing with these passages on asking prayer. As soon as they read this little addendum on abidance that Jesus set forth, thoughts immediately arise of all their faults and failures. Most assume these personal struggles have disqualified them in some way and this is why their prayers are not being answered. At this point, many believers just stop praying. They give up.

I understand this. Discouragement is a massive prayer killer. What I don't understand is why so many people I pastor and disciple see the cessation of prayer as the only answer to this conundrum.

It is rare to meet someone who, instead of backing off from prayer when discouraged, dives deeper into bold and audacious prayer. Continued prayer during seasons of discouragement is a sign of spiritual maturity. It means understanding the scriptural truth of your position as a son or daughter of the Most High and truly believing it. Few believers can look at the deficiencies in their spiritual lives without feeling rejected by God. It is like there is a God circle. When they sin or fail, they see themselves as being outside of that circle. When they succeed spiritually, they view themselves as again favored by God. This is not only scripturally unsound, but it demeans the power of what Christ did on the cross.

HOW TO BE A FRUIT-PRODUCING BRANCH

I imagine if you are reading this book, then you want to be a branch that produces fruit. You don't pick up books on bold and audacious asking prayer if you don't want to experience God's work in your life.

As a branch, you have a unique role. Branches are the conduits of nourishment for the production of fruit. This means you are the one responsible for sourcing nourishment to the fruit of your life. If you don't source it, your fruit will be unnourished, dry up, and die. Strategic and specific prayer keeps the fruit of your life healthy and vibrant. **Prayer directly transfers the sap of God's will, intention, and power to the fruit of your life and ministry.** Again, God allows us the freedom to decide how much fruit will be produced in our lives.

God wants to partner with us to build His kingdom and produce His fruit, but it is not a necessity. God can and does supply other branches to bear the fruit we have failed to produce. The simple fact is that this fruit will be produced; whether we produce it is up to us. Many believers give away bountiful harvests regularly trying to produce fruit on their own and apart from God. If we don't produce the fruit we are called to yield, God will use someone else to produce or harvest it.

Like spring rains, prayer calls forth the dormant seedlings of God's will and purpose and activates them. Many of these seedlings would remain dormant if not for the power of activating asking prayer. This is because God is willing to suppress His will if we choose not to collaborate with Him in bringing it forth.

In the first Psalm we see a road map for living this abiding and fruit-producing life: "Blessed is the man [person] who walks not in the counsel of the wicked, nor stands in the way of sinners, nor sits in the seat of scoffers; but his delight is in the law of the LORD, and on his law he meditates day and night. He is like a tree planted by streams of water that yields its fruit in its season, and its leaf does not wither. In all that he does, he prospers" (Ps. 1:1–3 ESV).

SOMETHING HAPPENS WHEN YOU ABIDE

Part of the blessing of the abiding life is knowing what God is calling us to do. Obviously, when we get to the business of doing what He wants us to do, we have a bountiful harvest in our lives. It's much easier to harvest when we know where the trees loaded with low-hanging fruit are located. Unfortunately, too many believers try to gather in the desert of their own striving.

This is the blessing of abiding and a product of showing up. I am fully convinced that much of abiding comes from showing up and making yourself present to God. When Jesus talks about praying for whatever we wish, He is assuming that prayer creation happens as a result of our time with God. **Time with God is the factory from which asking prayer is produced.**

This is a massive truth you don't want to miss. In order to understand the prayers God wants you to pray, you need to spend time with Him before you begin to pray those specific and strategic prayers into reality. Effectual asking prayer is a substance that can be created only by first spending time in God's unhindered presence.

This can happen in a number of ways. When we worship God, spend time in thanksgiving, meditate on His Word, or simply be still in His presence, we are working in the factory of prayer creation. Here God begins to fashion within us an understanding of the way in which He wants us to pray—things He will respond to. The more you know what to pray, the more you will experience the dramatic work of God in your life. You will always be working toward something of eternal value rather than striving after an eternity of nothing.

CHAPTER 8

EXTRA-VIRGIN

It has to do with seeing God. "Blessed are the pure in
heart, for they shall see God" (Matthew 5:8).

—John Piper

In this chapter I want to look at one of the most powerful tools at our
disposal to not only maintain deeper abidance but also release herds
of elephants into our lives. That tool is holiness.

Sometimes it seems that the only place our culture values purity
is in its olive oil. Recently some of the world's most renowned olive
oil connoisseurs met to discuss the ever-growing problem of olive oil
fraud.[1] Apparently, the world of black market olive oil trafficking is
fraught with danger and intrigue. Who knew?

What they found was that over half the olive oil that is mar-
keted as "extra-virgin" around the world has actually been sullied
in some way. I never understood the term *extra-virgin*. How exactly
does something become more virginal? It's kind of like being a bit
pregnant. You either are or you are not ... but I digress.

One of the problems with artificial extra-virgin olive oil is that it is hard to test for. Like the boutique and designer steroid market that permeates professional sports, oils of nefarious origin are getting better and better at avoiding detection. Things like chemical rather than natural extraction, which results in non-olive oils blending in to the final product, and the use of perfumes to hide rancidity disqualify oils from being termed "extra-virgin."

Like additives tainting olive oil, sinful contaminants are always blending in and tempting the church to sully her purity and derail her purpose. Take the church's fascination with being "authentic." Today the value of authenticity trumps the value of holiness. Giving in to sin is just you being who you are. We are told to accept everyone for who they decide they are or want to be while giving a free pass to their decisions or actions. Withholding from sinful action is increasingly seen as denying who we were created to be. God forbid we should ever deny ourselves anything.

Concurrently, there is also an uprising and interest in the work of the Holy Spirit. Many churches today are pursuing the power of the Spirit with a relentless passion. This is a worthy pursuit, but what we need to realize is that we cannot separate holiness from the Spirit. The things of the Spirit do not come devoid of purity. We can't have all the Spirit has to offer while casting the holy part aside.

OIL AND WATER

Like oil and water, prayer and sin don't mix. Similar to the impurities that destroy the quality of truly virgin olive oil, the sin that gets infused into our lives destroys the effectiveness of our prayers and purpose in life. **Sin is a prayer and purpose killer.**

Sin hampers prayer in two primary ways. The first is that when most people are entangled in sin, they simply stop praying because of guilt. Unfortunately, the answer to many people's struggles in prayer is the cessation of praying. Next, as Scripture demonstrates, sin seems to have the ability to clog prayer from its intention and power. One of many examples of this is found in the first book of Peter: "You husbands in the same way, live with your wives in an understanding way, as with someone weaker, since she is a woman; and show her honor as a fellow heir of the grace of life, so that your prayers will not be hindered" (1 Pet. 3:7 NASB).

In this verse, Peter made it pretty clear that treating your wife with a lack of respect will cause drag on your prayers. While Peter did not say whether they are merely hindered or blocked altogether, the point is still made that you can increase or decrease the effectiveness of your prayers by the way you treat your wife. I would imagine that this verse could be applied to the way you treat people in general; although Peter did not say this specifically, the books of John talk about this issue as part of the abiding process.

Here are some other biblical references that illustrate how sin puts the effectiveness of our prayers into captivity:

> If I had cherished sin in my heart, the Lord would not have listened. (Ps. 66:18)

> But your iniquities have made a separation between you and your God, and your sins have hidden His

face from you so that He does not hear. (Isa. 59:2
NASB)

"Get on your knees and pray that I will be gracious
to you. You priests have gotten everyone in trouble.
With this kind of conduct, do you think I'll pay
attention to you?" GOD-of-the-Angel-Armies asks
you. (Mal. 1:9 MSG)

You ask and do not receive, because you ask wrongly,
to spend it on your passions. (James 4:3 ESV)

PRAYER AND SIN

Ceasing to pray is never the answer to your struggles in prayer. If
you have things in your life that hinder your prayers, the best place to
start is with prayer. Prayer is always the answer to that which ails us.
The problems you experience in prayer are solved only one way—by
praying about them.

We alienate ourselves from God's voice and intentions when we
get caught up in sin. But God's answer to sin is grace, not rejection.
Romans 5:8 speaks to this when it declares that while we were still
deep in sin, Christ died for us. When we find ourselves mired in sin,
we need to accept the primary plan made available to us by God
Himself. This plan is grace. Grace begs us to submit to it when we are
in sin. Grace is a magnet for those who sin, not a ghastly brute to be
faced. When you are struggling with sin, the thing to do is show up
and meet with God in prayer. Jesus did not die on the cross so that

when you sin you run away and hide from Him. This was Adam and Eve's response of shame in the garden. Life after the cross calls the sinner to run home and rest in the arms of a loving Father, not hide naked and ashamed in the bushes. If you are feeling lost in sin, the place to start is by coming home in prayer.

With that said, I want to challenge you. If you have a problem with a certain sin in your life, it needs to be dealt with. Not only will grace give you freedom from the self-induced guilt that comes with sin, but it will unleash God's kingdom power into your life, as holiness is nuclear in the way it empowers prayer. Holiness extends the reach of your prayers. Holiness, like the kind found in the lives of biblical champions Joshua and Daniel, extends the reach of your entire life and thrusts you into the land of your promise. Let's take a look at how these two men's commitments to holiness shaped not only their prayers but also the entirety of their purposes.

CONSECRATE YOURSELF

Most of us want to live lives of purpose, lives of deep meaning. We want to see God do amazing things among us. After forty years of wandering in the desert, the children of Israel were tired of the mediocrity that came with living bland spiritual lives. They were ready for a change, ready to cross their Jordan and begin living in the land of their promise.

God's call to Joshua was to lead these people into their inheritance. (See Josh. 1:6.) If you remember from the story, Joshua was one of the original spies sent into the land by Moses to scope it out for the taking. (See Num. 13:1–2.) Of the twelve spies that Moses sent, only Joshua and Caleb had the faith to believe in the promise of God. The remaining ten spies melted with fear upon seeing the giants in the land. (See Num. 13:28.) Because of this sin of unbelief, the entire nation would be hindered in the taking of their promise and the capturing of the land that God had intended for them. As a result of the sin of faithlessness, Israel as a nation would have to wait forty extra years before taking the land. This is because sin has the ability to detour us from our purposes. It is possible that some of the elephants you have been praying for would be released by a personal commitment to holiness. As mentioned, this was the case with the Israelites and their Promised Land.

When Israel did enter the land, only those under military age at the time of their unfaithfulness would enter the land of promise with Joshua and Caleb. (See Josh. 5:6.) The rest would die wandering in the desert and never claim their inheritance.

Fast-forward forty years. Now Joshua was somewhere between sixty and eighty years of age and finally rallying the troops for a long-awaited possession of the land. This time Joshua would not allow sin to hinder his people's progress.

While Joshua understood all the provisions needed for a journey of this magnitude, he was most concerned with the one commodity that would most affect the success or failure of this expedition—holiness. Joshua said, "Consecrate yourselves, for tomorrow the LORD will do *amazing things* among you" (Josh. 3:5).

Simply put, amazing things follow holiness. As Joshua found out, nothing could stop God's power and purpose for Israel when they were walking in step with His ways. If you want to see God do amazing things in your life, you need to consecrate yourself.

You need to take stock of your life and extricate from it the things that hold you back. You need to rid yourself of the poison of sinful actions. You need to want more than just enough holiness to release the tension of guilt that plagues you. You need to end the excuses and rationalization for the things you are doing and remember one key truth. If it needs to be explained and rationalized, it's probably not holiness.

STARTING POINT

The starting point for the consecration of your life is prayer. It is going boldly before the throne of God and exposing your wounds to Jesus. We tend to forget that Jesus made it His practice to touch the leper's wounds. (See Mark 1:41.) If you show Jesus your wounds, He will touch them. In prayer we expose our wounds of sinfulness to God and say things like, "God, I am infatuated with this sin. It has overcome me. I confess that I don't even want to give it up. I pray You would give me the desire to want to stop." Again, prayer is the starting point of consecration. Prayer to conquer the sin that besieges you should be near the top of your elephant list of prayers.

The next step to consecrating yourself before God is right action. Just do the right thing. It's a basic concept. Call a friend for accountability and out yourself. Throw the bottle of pills into the toilet and burn the stash of pornography. Call the person you have not forgiven and forgive him or her. Stop the gossip and return the thing you stole. Holiness is as simple as doing the right thing in this moment.

The importance of this cannot be overstated. Holiness unlocks doors of purpose in your life a lot faster than any to-do list or seminars and books on purpose-filled living can. **If you commit to living in holiness, your purpose will hunt you down and lie at your feet.**

The elephant of purpose is something I am going to dig into deeply as we come in for a landing on this book. Few elephants in our lives rank as high on our lists as our individual purpose and search for meaning do.

DANIEL'S PRAYER LIFE

Daniel was a man who experienced the power of holiness and its effect on his prayers. In the example of Joshua, we saw how holiness opened up access to the crossing of his and Israel's collective Jordan. The Jordan was the barrier that stood between them and their purpose. Once they were consecrated and walking in holiness, the barrier of the Jordan River that stood between them and the land of their calling was divided. They crossed through the waters and into their identity.

Prayer is the road on which our personal purpose travels. If your purpose and calling were a vehicle traveling to its destination, your prayers steeped in holiness would be the smooth pavement on which it would travel. This is just as true for the other elephants that you are praying for. Prayer combined with holy living can catapult the intent of those prayers into immediate play. We see this in the fascinating account of Daniel's interaction with the archangel Michael.

In Daniel 9 we read about Daniel coming before the Lord in a prayer of confession. Daniel praying over the sins of Israel and asking that God restore not only the temple but the entire nation to its right standing. Daniel used prayer as the starting place of a deep commitment to holiness. You can do the same.

> In the first year of Darius son of Xerxes (a Mede by descent), who was made ruler over the Babylonian kingdom—in the first year of his reign, I, Daniel, understood from the Scriptures, according to the word of the LORD given to Jeremiah the prophet, that the desolation of Jerusalem would last seventy years. So I turned to the Lord God and pleaded with him in prayer and petition, in fasting, and in sackcloth and ashes.
>
> I prayed to the LORD my God and confessed:
>
> "Lord, the great and awesome God, who keeps his covenant of love with those who love him and keep his commandments, we have sinned and done wrong. We have been wicked and have rebelled; we have turned away from your commands and laws. We have not listened to your servants the prophets, who spoke in your name to our kings, our princes and our ancestors, and to all the people of the land."
>
> (Dan. 9:1–6)

While we could spend a thousand pages pressing into all that this passage has to offer, I want to keep this as straightforward and simple as possible. Daniel recognized sin and confessed it. Not only did he confess it, but he let God know that he was serious in his intent by tagging his prayers with fasting, sackcloth, and ash. Both of these actions by Daniel were for the sole purpose of humbling himself before God.

The immediate response by God to the humble and consecrated prayers of Daniel is something we must take note of and not undersell. I believe nothing gets our prayers into immediate play like humility, confession, and deliberate holiness.

> While I was speaking and praying, confessing my sin and the sin of my people Israel and making my request to the LORD my God for his holy hill—*while I was still in prayer*, Gabriel, the man I had seen in the earlier vision, came to me in *swift flight* about the time of the evening sacrifice. He instructed me and said to me, "Daniel, I have now come to give you insight and understanding. As soon as you began to pray, a word went out, which I have come to tell you, for you are highly esteemed. Therefore, consider the word and understand the vision." (Dan. 9:20–23)

I love how God was so excited to get to the business of responding to the prayers of Daniel that He did not even wait for him to finish his sentence. Rather, God immediately sent the archangel Gabriel in swift flight to address Daniel's concern. This is a powerful lesson and illustrates that God does not need us to craft perfect and complete times of prayer for Him to act in power. God moved on the prayers of Daniel before they had even left his lips. God was looking at the intent of Daniel's heart. Once He gazed upon Daniel's desolation of self-will and humility, He rushed to respond. This same concept is found in the writings of Isaiah, where it says, "It will also come to pass that before they call, I will answer; and while they are still speaking, I will hear" (Isa. 65:24 NASB).

Let me assure you that God is eager to respond to your request. As a matter of fact, He already died so that He could respond beyond what was possible in the days of Daniel. With that said, God is also willing to hinder His response to our prayers when we live in a way that does not abide with His decrees. God does not require perfection; that was the job of His Son. What God does require is regular confession and a commitment to do our best to live in holiness.

YOU PROBABLY DON'T QUALIFY

Let's return to that laundry list of sin and shame that will keep your prayers from being answered. While I would love to write a feel-good book and avoid all these tensions, I cannot. The truth of God's Word is balanced and requires us to look at both sides of the coin.

Passages like the ones listed earlier about sin and prayer can seem like giants in the land of our prayer lives. Like the giants mentioned throughout the Old Testament, these verses can taunt and tempt us to cease chasing after a life in Christ because of shame and guilt when manipulated by the Enemy.

Take for instance James's harsh tones about our motives in James 4:3. For years this verse was a prayer killer for me. It kept me from praying for many fun and perhaps extravagant requests. Many of these I have mentioned in the previous chapters. I thought that I should never pray for anything that was strictly meant for my own enjoyment. It seemed that God had something against pleasure for pleasure's sake.

And James did not stop there. Don't forget what he wrote in James 1:6. Here, if you have the slightest amount of doubt when you pray, then you are lumped in with the double minded and scolded with threats of never seeing your elephants come home.

When coming to any of the conditional verses on prayer, like the ones I just mentioned, we need to make sure that we not only understand the context in which they were written but also juxtapose them against the rest of Scripture. Let's again take a look at James through these lenses:

> What causes fights and quarrels among you? Don't they come from your desires that battle within you? You desire but do not have, so you kill. You covet but you cannot get what you want, so you quarrel and fight. You do not have because you do not ask God. When you ask, you do not receive, because you ask with wrong motives, that you may spend what you get on your pleasures.
>
> You adulterous people, don't you know that friendship with the world means enmity against God? Therefore, anyone who chooses to be a friend of the world becomes an enemy of God. Or do you think Scripture says without reason that he jealously longs for the spirit he has caused to dwell in us? But he gives us more grace. That is why Scripture says:

"God opposes the proud
but shows favor to the humble."
(James 4:1–6)

If we focus only on verse 1, it is really easy to get tripped up. We don't want to pray in selfish ways that displease God. This makes sense. But as we move further down the passage, we see that James is not addressing the average believer but rather those who have turned from friendship with God to the ways of the world. Of course, if we are adulterous murderers who care about nothing but our own pleasure, God will have a problem with us. My point is that you probably don't qualify for the intent of this passage nor as a member of James's intended audience.

We can still learn from these verses, however, as all of Scripture is beneficial for our edification. (See 2 Tim. 3:16.) Yes, we need to make sure that our prayer times are not focused solely on our own pleasure and wants; but with that said, we must also realize that many of the verses I've listed in this section were written to people who had for the most part abandoned their faith.

INTEGRITY

In 1994 at the National Youth Workers Convention held in San Francisco, I sat under the teaching of a man who had lost his integrity. That man was Richard Dortch. If you remember the eighties, then you most likely recall that Dortch was a former executive of PTL (Praise the Lord), the Christian television ministry, whose life and ministry had crashed when the organization and its founder, Jim

Bakker, were brought down during the Jessica Hahn sex and financial scandal that rocked not only the church but American culture.

From the pulpit that day, Dortch recounted the story of years of spotless ministry that all went bad over a three-year period when his public persona failed to match his private one. Dortch, now free from serving his prison term, was traveling the country making amends and preaching the message of personal integrity.

I have never forgotten this flagship message. It is in my ten most memorable sermons, and it has served as a rudder that has guided many of my decisions over the last twenty years of life and ministry.

As we close this chapter, I feel impressed to share a few of the things Richard Dortch said. The first is that massive personal failure does not come overnight. Rather, it is earned through a slow and progressive departure from what you know as truth. I remember him saying that stealing millions of dollars from an organization begins by taking things like paper clips home from the office that you know don't belong to you.

Next, the restored pastor said, "The best metaphor for integrity is glass. Glass is solid in structure, but clear. If one looks at glass, it can be seen through. Is your life able to be seen through?"

Just a few moments before Dortch left the stage that day, he concluded by saying that when he got to the federal penitentiary, he was surprised to find that eight other pastors were also behind those bars with him. I have always remembered this and prayed to God that by His grace and a commitment to personal holiness, I would never join them.

My hope in adding this section to the end of this chapter on holiness and prayer is to perhaps save a few marriages, lives, businesses, and ministries from shipwreck. If you are currently in a place where the windowpane of your life is not clear, but rather murky and covered in haze, the place to start is with prayer. Pray not only for repentance but that God would give you the courage to regain your integrity no matter what the cost. Only in this way, after being pressed in the vat of God's truth and integrity, will the life you live be truly labeled extra-virgin. The book of James says:

> Is anyone among you in trouble? Let them pray. Is anyone happy? Let them sing songs of praise. Is anyone among you sick? Let them call the elders of the church to pray over them and anoint them with oil in the name of the Lord. And the prayer offered in faith will make the sick person well; the Lord will raise them up. If they have sinned, they will be forgiven. Therefore confess your sins to each other and pray for each other so that you may be healed. The prayer of a righteous person is powerful and effective. (James 5:13–16)

CHAPTER 9

BE THE ANSWER

*Pray as though everything depended on God. Work
as though everything depended on you.*

—Saint Augustine

Either we believe prayer is real, powerful, and of eternal significance,
or we think it is a fool's superstition. There is no middle ground.
Unfortunately, many of us live and pray as if there is. We may accept
prayer's ability to shape our destinies as a premise, but when it comes
to the brass tacks of real world living, prayer places a distant finisher
to our personal abilities to create and control our own paths.

In the past, much of society viewed faith in God and especially
the religious practice of prayer as taking part in ultimate reality.
Those who practiced the life of faith and prayer with authentic fervor
were considered the most real people in the world. Prayer was God's
tool placed into the hands of mankind for the purpose of saturating
the eternal realities of heaven into the transitory and mortal world
of now.

In Western culture, superstition has largely been seen as in a separate camp of belief from traditional religious practice. Superstitious people don't step on cracks in the sidewalk or walk under ladders, and they believe in characters like Shakespeare's forest fairy Puck.

Today the gap between what was once viewed as authentic faith and that of fool's superstition is closing. When Noah Webster defined *superstition* in 1828, he saw it as "excess and extravagance in religion" and "the doing of things not required by God." This second component, the part about things not required by God, clearly shows that in Webster's time, there was a valid form of faith not associated with superstition.

Compare this to *Wikipedia's* most modern definition. *Superstition* is deemed a pejorative term for "belief in *supernatural causality*."[1] The definition goes on to list religion in general as an example along with witchcraft, omens, and astrology. The needle has shifted.

The term *supernatural causality* may be impressive to use in dinner conversations, but it also has a profound impact on the way you view God's ability to shape and change your life. *Supernatural causality* means something outside of the natural world has the ability to shape or cause things to happen within it. An example would be praying that God would get your kid into a certain teacher's class. Most people of faith pray and believe prayer has the ability to change outcomes. Sadly, by today's secular standard, if you pray believing in supernatural causality, then you most likely also look for trolls living under bridges.

In this modern world, what you can see and prove trumps that which is unseen. What you can touch is real; what you cannot touch doesn't exist. The world is now said to have been set in motion and only natural causes affect outcomes. Without empirical proof to the contrary, any tree that falls in the forest without a witness makes no sound, and any prayer prayed to an invisible God goes unheard.

THE SUPERSTITION OF FAITH

What the world now calls superstition, the Bible calls faith. In the eleventh chapter of the book of Hebrews it says, "Now faith is the *reality* of what is hoped for, the *proof* of what is not seen" (Heb. 11:1 HCSB).

What the writer of Hebrews is saying is that faith is not something that will be proven true once all things are revealed, but rather that faith is the living, breathing proof that you can touch and experience in the present. Faith is to the modern believer what the actual wounds of Christ were to the apostle Thomas. (See John 20:24–29.)

Other translations of Scripture use the words "substance" or "reality" when describing faith.[2] The point is that faith is not some invisible thought or emotion but rather as tangible as solid ground.

The more you pray, the more you will live in and experience this true reality. This is because it is impossible to pray without faith. The fact that you are praying at all means you have faith that someone is listening. The more you focus on and chase the things of this world that are passing away, the less reality you will experience. How can this be? It's pretty simple. The things that last forever are more real than the things that will pass away. The apostle Paul said, "And now these three remain: faith, hope and love. But the greatest of these is love" (1 Cor. 13:13).

Now that we have established that prayer makes you more real in this life by blending the lasting things of eternity into the present, we need to take it to the next level. What I find strange is that so many believers have the faith to pray to God but then stumble when it comes to believing in the power or ability of those prayers to make a difference. This is like having the faith to jump over the Grand Canyon but doubting you can clear the small gap between the subway and platform. Believing in God at all is a much bigger leap than believing that He hears and acts when you pray to Him.

Perhaps you have heard the British phrase "Mind the gap." It refers to the perilous eight inches between the train and the platform in the London metro system. It is a small gap, but if it is not minded, you will end up incapacitated with one leg in the car and one between it and the platform.

Even today I struggle with this gap of faith. Do I really believe that my prayers can cause things to happen? I am still regularly tempted with the thought that God is sovereign and He will have His way regardless of my prayers, so what's the point?

I believe this is a half-truth. Yes, God is completely sovereign and will have His way in the end, but perhaps there are different paths in which He can work out His ultimate conclusions. Does God leave Himself margin to move and adjust within His grand endgame? The French philosopher Blaise Pascal said yes and called this "the dignity of causality." What he meant was that God has multiple ways to accomplish His ultimate will and those who submit themselves to it will through prayer open up to the possibility of being part of the path to that end. Like many roads to a particular destination, all will lead to their intended purpose, but perhaps God would let you ride shotgun on a particular journey if you asked in prayer. We see an example of this idea of causality in the book of Ezekiel when it says, "I searched for a man among them who would build up the wall and stand in the gap before Me for the land, so that I would not destroy it; but I found no one" (Ezek. 22:30 NASB).

If we are to accept this verse at face value, it means that God was on the lookout for someone He could collaborate with in the salvation of an entire land. Either God was authentically looking for someone to partner with in releasing His kingdom on earth, or He was using poetic and metaphorical language just to increase literary tension. The way you interpret this scripture and others like it will largely dictate your belief on prayerful causality. It will also dictate how much God uses you in the particular working out of His kingdom building. The more you pray, the more you will be used.

PANCAKES WITH GOD

I love the idea of being a coconspirator with God. It reminds me of making pancakes with my seven-year-old daughter, Lucy. Growing up in the restaurant business, I learned to cook at a very young age. While I'm not a master chef, I can hold my own in the kitchen. The ritual of Saturday pancake breakfast in our home is more art than proletariat function. I make a bananas Foster pancake to die for.

Usually, before I even reach for the flour, Lucy asks me if she can be part of the action. Immediately, she begins to pepper me with new ideas for pancake variations. "How about chocolate chips and peanut butter, Dad?" or "What about blueberries with strawberry syrup?" Lucy loves to be in the mix.

Here's the point. Pancakes are going to be made that day. Whether Lucy conspires to help me or not is up to her. On the days she does, the pancakes not only take on an entirely different direction, but Lucy gets to experience the dignity of causality. She gets to exclaim to her mom and big sister, Lily, "Look what Dad and I made." She also gets the satisfaction of savoring the final product knowing she had a hand in creating it. This is how I believe and have experienced prayer to work. After the cake is baked, we exclaim in praise and thanksgiving, "Look what my dad and I made!"

In C. S. Lewis's short essay titled "The Efficacy of Prayer," Lewis spoke about a day he was going to get a haircut but decided against it as his day began to unfold. Suddenly, he had an "unaccountable nagging voice" in his head that suggested he get this haircut after all. Following that soul tug and upon arriving at the shop, the barber told him that he had been praying earlier in the day that Lewis would come in for a haircut. Lewis explained it this way:

> It awed me; it awes me still. But of course one cannot rigorously prove a causal connection between the barber's prayers and my visit. It might be telepathy. It might be accident.
>
> The question then arises, "What sort of evidence *would* prove the efficacy [the ability to produce a desired or intended result] of prayer?" The thing we pray for may happen, but how can

you ever know it was not going to happen anyway? Even if the thing were indisputably miraculous it would not follow that the miracle had occurred because of your prayers. The answer surely is that a compulsive empirical proof such as we have in the sciences can never be attained.

But not only prayer; whenever we act at all He lends us that dignity [the dignity of causality]. It is not really stranger, nor less strange, that my prayers should affect the course of events than that my other actions should do so. They have not advised or changed God's mind—that is, His over-all purpose. But that purpose will be realized in different ways according to the actions, including the prayers, of His creatures.[3]

William Temple said it another way: "When I pray, coincidences happen, and when I don't pray, they don't."

Billy Graham spoke to making pancakes with God like this: "Heaven is full of answers to prayers for which no one ever bothered to ask."

As Lewis suggested, the ability to prove this point or the efficacy of prayer at all for that matter is impossible. Perhaps the pancake is already fried and just waiting to be enjoyed at the great and coming wedding feast foretold in the book of Revelation. If this is the case, I am fine with it. I trust God. But what if this understanding of prayer's ability to collaborate with God in not only creating your future life but perhaps altering the course of human history is the way God actually works? What if you get to heaven and see all the things God wanted to do in your life, but you missed out in this present reality simply because you failed to ask? What if without a William Wilberforce or Abraham Lincoln boldly asking for the abolition of slavery it might still exist today? What if?

BE GOD'S ANSWER

Few things allow us to be God's answers to the problems of the world like prayer does. When we pray, God sets to the work of answering our petitions, but prayer also establishes within us an understanding of what God wants done in the world and begs us to enter into the action beyond just praying. **Prayer is the crossroads of faith and action.**

Prayer's dualistic call is not only to God but also to us as a community of believers to respond in partnership with God. We are called to pray for our elephants, but we are also called to hunt them down through our own Spirit-led actions.

While I agree that God occasionally calls us to pray and asks us to wait in faith-filled inaction, I do not believe this is the general command of Scripture. The Bible more often than not is a book that calls its hearers to action. Many times the Word tells us to wait, but often it also commands us to go. Does the Great Commission tell us to wait for disciples to come to us? No, it commands us to go and become God's answer to the lost. The original disciples did not pray for the salvation of the entire world and then sit on their hands in Jerusalem. Yes, they waited for a time and to be equipped, but then they went and became the living, breathing answer to their prayers. Most of them gave their lives in martyrdom to become that answer.

The same is true for us. We are called not only to pray but to prayerfully act. While I am not encouraging you to strive in your own flesh, I am saying that many of your prayers should have hands and feet attached to them. Those hands and feet belong to you.

Jesus's call to pray for whatever we are willing to pray for comes with an ancillary call to also work at becoming the answer to those prayers. In this way we hold firmly to the reality of faith's substance. Like Abraham before us, we are called to take steps in the direction of God's leading while holding on to our faith the entire time. The book of Genesis says, "Now Jehovah said unto Abram, Get thee out of thy country, and from thy kindred, and from thy father's house, unto the land that I will show thee" (Gen. 12:1 ASV). Abraham's story is picked up again in the book of Hebrews and points to Abraham's obedience when it says, "By faith Abraham, when called to go to a place he would later receive as his inheritance, obeyed and went, even though he did not know where he was going" (Heb. 11:8).

The point is that Abraham's feet walked him directly into his promise through faith-filled action. The same will be true for us when we step out in the Spirit-led pursuit of our prayers rather than sit on the sidelines of faith waiting for God to do it all.

GO WHERE THE ELEPHANTS ARE

A few weeks ago, a friend of mine was giving me a hard time about my elephant story. He told me that it was not that big of a miracle that I found an elephant in Thailand. He said the story would have had more impact if the elephant had come to my home in Orange County. While he was only joking, it caused me to think. The more

I thought about his comment, the more I began to disagree. You find elephants by going to the place where elephants are. If you want to find an elephant, you will have a much better chance in India and Africa than you will in Poland or Finland.

This is a precept that the early church understood. Not only did they pray for elephants, but they were willing to go to the places where elephants lived. Often their actions embodied the very elephant others were praying for. Here is what I mean.

Like our churches today, the first-century church was full of need. There were widows and orphans to be looked after, believers in extreme poverty, and of course, the sick and infirm who needed care. The following verse points to these needs and how the early church responded to them: "Everyone around was in awe—all those wonders and signs done through the apostles! And all the believers lived in a wonderful harmony, holding everything in common. They sold whatever they owned and pooled their resources so that each person's need was met" (Acts 2:43–45 MSG).

The early church was filled with need, but the majority of those needs were met by the very people who were praying for help. (See Acts 6:1–4; 2 Cor. 8:1–5.) The early church would pray, and then they would go about the business of being the answer to those prayers by living in benevolent and servant-like ways.

This is a crucial part of understanding the message of the elephant. I believe that the majority of elephants we and those around us are praying for are ours for the taking if we, like the first-century church, are willing to step out and claim them.

This means not only praying that homeless people will be well fed and kept warm but actually giving them blankets and meals. It means giving financially to the future missionary in your church whose biggest elephant is to enter the foreign missionary field. Or perhaps it means being the elephant of the orphan in foster care praying for a family to call her own.

I think this was what James was getting at when he wrote about faith and action. Prayer is a major platform of faith, and like faith, our prayers are often validated in the action that accompanies our petitions. James said, "What good is it, my brothers and sisters, if someone claims to have faith but has no deeds? Can such faith save them? Suppose a brother or a sister is without clothes and daily food. If one of you says to them, 'Go in peace; keep warm and well fed,' but does nothing about their physical needs, what good is it?" (James 2:14–16).

I think one could just as easily say, what good is it if you pray but have no deeds? Is prayer not one of the most dynamic platforms where our faith is put on display? Should we pray for the homeless and not collect blankets to keep them warm? When we pray for a family who is going through cancer, do we also give toward their medical bills? One of the best practices you can implement into your following of Jesus is that when you tell people you will pray for them, follow up that commitment by asking what you can do for them in the moment. Ask them how you can help be their elephant in the present.

DISNEYLAND AND ANSWERED PRAYER

A few weeks ago a woman posted on the Praying for Your Elephant social media page that she was praying for the opportunity to take her daughter to Disneyland for her sixth birthday but could not afford it. As usual with requests like this that are posted on the site, she included a note about feeling foolish praying for this request but had done so after speaking with me and being encouraged to post it. As you know by now, I'm not a big fan of editing prayer requests because of guilt.

What happened next was awesome. Within a couple of hours someone had posted that she had bought her and her daughter passes to Disneyland and wanted to know how to deliver them. Granted, this is not the end of world hunger, but it is the church being the church she is called to be and it puts her beauty on display.

This act of benevolence on our Facebook group prayer page encouraged a flurry of other people to step up to be the answer to other people's elephants. One woman needed prayer for a sore neck, and right away another women, one of our professional masseuses, offered her a free hour-long massage. Another person posted a prayer need for an automobile that someone responded to with the offer to lend that person a car.

I call these people—people who respond to other people's prayers—elephant hunters. Those who subscribe to the Praying for Your Elephant prayer cast know exactly what I am talking about, and it has become the mission of many to actively seek out where they can be the answers to other people's prayers.

The simple takeaway is this. Prayer is not a static commodity to be left to its own devices once uttered. Rather, prayer is the starting line of God's kingdom work on earth. Yes, Abraham Lincoln prayed; that is something history has recorded in detail. What made men like Lincoln and England's Wilberforce different was that after they prayed, they went out and did something courageous to see those prayers come about. In a sense, they became the answer to what they prayed for. If you want to live an eternally empowered kingdom life, pray and then go and become the answer to those prayers through the empowering of Christ Jesus. Be the answer. Be the elephant!

WHEN ELEPHANTS CHARGE

Had to let you know how grateful I am that we talked today. As I mentioned, my husband has been ill and not able to work. After we spoke I sent an email to the woman you suggested could help us and she called me shortly afterward. Then she went right to work and within a couple of hours I had checks for the mortgage, truck, and phone payments. I am still in shock!! I know God is good but this is crazy (but a good kind of crazy).

Yesterday I had asked a few close friends to pray for our situation. One of them texted me, "I am praying for more than you could ask or imagine." I was delighted to be able to share with her how her prayer had been answered.

Some days I feel like we are getting hit in every direction. But then I go to the basics of prayer and Bible reading and I am encouraged. Today God blew my mind.

Thank you for all your faithfulness in keeping up with our family!

Blessings!

Lynda

CHAPTER 10

ELEPHANT WORSHIP

Dear children, keep yourselves from idols.
—1 John 5:21

In 2009 a frumpy middle-aged woman waddled onto the stage of a popular English television talent show and was asked by one of the judges a question that is central to the human heart, a question central to human existence. He asked, "What's the dream?"

The woman sheepishly exclaimed that she dreamed to be a singer who might someday be as popular as Elaine Paige. It was a modest request by big dream standards, as few people even know who Elaine Paige is these days.

Like sharks to a feeding frenzy, a merciless audience began to chuckle and laugh, greedily anticipating the coming epic failure. Blood was in the water, and shows like this are just as much about people with real talent as they are about others making fools of themselves in front of national audiences.

The tension in the room thickened as the woman revealed her song choice for the evening. It was "I Dreamed a Dream" from the epic musical *Les Misérables*, an ambitious selection for even the most talented of singers.

The producers of the show could not have been more elated. It was a perfect song for an occasion such as this. Tonight, on live TV, this woman's dreams would be turned to shame in front of a nation for the sake of ratings. Tonight another dream would be put to death.

Then magic happened.

What played out that night after Susan Boyle began to sing is the stuff that dreams are made of. Granted, Boyle is an incredibly God-gifted singer, and there are a lot of fantastic singers in the world, but few go on to become overnight, worldwide, and viral Internet sensations. Something deeper happened on the stage that night, something transcendent, something that spoke a whisper into the depths of people's beings. This was the story of the underdog, the dark horse who came from behind in a race that for her was surely over. It was the British version of the American dream.

The reason that Boyle's performance so moved a world was that it touched something God-given and powerful in all of us: the desire to see our dreams realized. And while we often hear stories of such things happening to people from afar, few times do we get to be firsthand witnesses to it.

DREAMING OF ELEPHANTS

When it comes to praying for elephants, perhaps nothing compares to the elephants of our personal purpose and dreams. These massive pachyderms stand out from all the other items we pray for. These are the elephants that we often measure our worth by. These are the elephants we will pray about for decades. These are the elephants that if found promise us happiness and contentment. And these are the elephants that if not kept in their proper place will tempt us, like the Hindu elephant god Ganesha, to fall down and worship at their feet.

As a pastor for almost two decades, I have had a front-row seat in the theater of people's dreams. I have seen them realized, and I have seen them dashed. Helping people shepherd their dreams is probably one of the most important aspects of my job. In modern Christian circles, our dreams are often intertwined with our understanding of God's will and purpose for our lives. Some Scripture verses have become modern platforms for pushing the agenda of personal purpose, individual fulfillment, and contentment. Take for example a verse from the Psalms, which says, "Delight yourself in the LORD, and he will give you the desires of your heart" (Ps. 37:4 ESV). Or consider the following verse from Jeremiah: "For I know the thoughts that I think toward you, saith the LORD, thoughts of peace, and not of evil, to give you an expected end" (Jer. 29:11 KJV).

The problem is that mixing this cocktail of personal dreams and desires with the actual will of God is tricky business and something nonreligious people do not suffer.

For the irreligious, the realization of dreams is often all about hard work mixed with a little bit of luck or fate. If your dreams fall flat on their faces, then they just were not meant to be. If your dreams are realized, then you can thank good fortune and elbow grease.

For the Christian, it is not that simple. We Christians often feel the need to analyze our dreams, to put them under the microscope and decide if they are really God's dreams for us. We have to ask if they are the kind of dreams God might be proud of. For instance, would the desire to be an artist or an Olympian or perhaps even a circus performer be a dream that God would value and bless?

What about when our dreams and elephants don't come to fruition in the way we planned or are lost altogether? Here at the junction of faith and broken dreams we often have to deal with a stout, self-induced guilt or doubt that creeps in and questions our standing with God. Have we done something wrong? Is there sin in our lives? Did we misunderstand what we thought God had told us? Is God mad at us? Maybe if we had prayed more, things would have been different.

Conversely, the same is true when our prayers for elephants are answered and our dreams seem to be on track, when we get that job or spouse that has for so long been the object of our desire. It is in these times that we are tempted to feel secure in God's love for us based on our current circumstance rather than the scriptural truth of God's complete and perfect love for His beloved children separate from dream fulfillment. The Bible is clear that nothing can separate us from the love of God. The book of Romans says, "For I am convinced that neither death, nor life, nor angels, nor rulers, nor things present, nor things to come, nor powers, nor height, nor depth, nor anything else in all creation, will be able to separate us from the love of God in Christ Jesus our Lord" (Rom. 8:38–39 NRSV). Feeling secure in God's love no matter what state your dreams are in is mature Christ following.

This modern knotting of our personal purpose and dreams with God's sovereign will has caused one of the greatest glacial shifts for individual believers since Adam and Eve ate the forbidden fruit. Consider this. Little more than a century ago, few followers of Christ had the option to even think of pursuing their dreams. Mostly they did what those before them had done. The bakers made bread, the smithies smote, and the Stadtmillers, as in my family's case, milled. Survival and duty were the keys to everyday life.

People still had dreams and desires back then, but fewer of them tied these dreams to their individual understanding of their position in Christ. Back then most believers did not have the luxury of worrying about whether their desired vocation or extracurricular pursuits put them smack-dab in the imaginary center of God's will. And that brings me to a key point. How can something eternal such as God's will have a center? No, in the past, the lion's share of believers spent most of their time worrying about things of greater consequence, things like, will the rains come this year to water our crops, or will my children escape polio?

The rise of an individual's ability to boldly pursue the elephants of their dreams, especially in Western cultures, has grown hand in hand with the prosperity that has befallen these civilizations. And this is a good thing, as dreams without the freedom and means to pursue them are often left unrealized. Dreams that have been submitted and surrendered to God are powerful kingdom stuff. God loves to run and play with us in the field of our dreams.

But turning our attention back to the believers who have lived and died on this earth before us, we must understand that few had the ability to engage in such pursuits. Take for instance Christian slaves in the first century. It is estimated that 30 percent of all Roman individuals were slaves.[1] Paul was aware of this when he wrote to them in Ephesians about how they were to be assured that they were living in accordance with God's will. He said:

> Slaves, obey your human masters with fear and trembling, in the sincerity of your heart, as to Christ. Don't work only while being watched, in order to please men, but as slaves of Christ, do God's will from your heart. Serve with a good attitude, as to the Lord and not to men, knowing that whatever good each one does, slave or free, he will receive this back from the Lord. (Eph. 6:5–8 HCSB)

If that is not dream-killing language, then I don't know what is. Paul suggested that if you were a slave, then you should obey your earthly master in the same way you would obey Jesus Himself and then be satisfied in knowing that you are living according to God's will.

While Paul was not advocating slavery in this verse, as some have suggested, he did understand that it was a part of the Roman culture in which he lived and it was probably not going to change anytime soon. What Paul was trying to accomplish in this verse was to give hope of a greater substance to people suffering under the bonds of slavery. Paul's message is that there is something more important than your circumstances and more important than your dreams.

Did Christian slaves in Rome have dreams of freedom and glories beyond servitude? Yes, to dream is to be human. Dreams flow from the creative nature God imprinted on His foremost creation—humans. But most of these early believers understood that their dreams would never be realized. Like mist over a loch, their dreams could be seen but never grasped.

How does that teaching strike you as a twenty-first-century modern? If Paul were to turn that perspective into a book today, it would not sell many copies. He probably could not even find an agent to shop the manuscript.

But if we are to take that ancient Pauline perspective at face value, then how relevant would our modern understanding of personal purpose and individual dream pursuit be to early believers? The answer is, not much.

Consider the bestselling Christian books of the last two decades. A great many of them are books about God enlarging personal territories and individual purposes. These are concepts that would not make much sense to so many of the believers who came before us or even modern-day Christians rummaging through the slums of Brazil and Africa trying to survive.

I am a firm believer that the core truths of Scripture must be true for all believers and not just a certain set, demographic, or millennia. And this is the truth of Scripture for all believers. Our greatest dream has already been realized in Jesus Christ. Nothing else compares.

YOUR GREATEST DREAM

Like many of you reading this book, I bought into "American dream" Christianity and have had to detoxify myself from it. When my dreams did not go the way I wanted them to, I became discouraged, distraught, and despairing. I'll talk about some of these struggles and how God taught me to surrender my dreams in the next chapter, "The Elephant Graveyard."

So how are you doing with those elephants that seem out of reach? I don't mean how are you going to be doing as soon as you get the thing you think you want, but how are you dealing with it right now? Is there a level of satisfaction and contentment in your life with what is right in front of you, or can satisfaction in Christ alone only happen once you get what you want? Do you view your life as having less meaning if your elephant never shows up?

Let me ask you a tougher question. It's a question that makes people put down books that don't make them feel good, but it is a question that must be asked. **Is Jesus alone enough for you?** I ask that question for all the people who have had to let go of their elephants for the sake of survival or duty. I ask it for all the single moms who have real talent beyond doing dishes and picking up soiled laundry but who work two waitressing jobs so their kids won't have to wear shoes with holes in them. I ask because I have a friend dying of cancer who might never see his kids grow up and who told me with the greatest of sincerity, "In the end I have discovered one thing through all of this. Jesus and cancer are enough."

What? Jesus and cancer are enough? That makes absolutely no sense to me. But when my friend said it with tears in his eyes and all the seriousness of a caged tiger, I knew he was on to something and he was experiencing life in Christ far beyond where I am currently living. He was speaking from the shadow lands of life in Christ. He was holding on to the only dream that mattered, the only dream that would survive. Jesus.

So what about you? Would Jesus and cancer be enough, or do you need all the accoutrements of blessing in your life to qualify Jesus for following with a glad and joyful heart?

What if your dreams never come true, your elephant never shows up? What if, like Moses, you spend a life following God through a host of deserts only to get to the edge of the Promised Land but never make it in? Is Jesus enough?

What if you stay single and never have that gaggle of kids you have so longed for? Is Jesus enough? What if your novel never gets published or your song never gets sung? Is Jesus enough? And for all of you who have wanted to go into full-time vocational ministry, what if you never get the ministry position of your dreams? What if you never make it to the mission field? Is Jesus enough?

Is Jesus enough?

Is Jesus enough?

Is Jesus enough?

This is not a book asking you to abandon your dreams—far from it. One of the passions of my life is helping people realize their dreams and pray boldly for their elephants. This book is all about your dreams and elephants, but it is asking you to put them in their proper place, to perhaps stop worshipping them. It is asking you to make them secondary and to replace them with a greater dream—Jesus. If Jesus alone is not enough for you, then nothing ever will be. But if, regardless of what comes next in life, Jesus alone is sufficient for you, then there will never be anything that can offer more satisfaction or steal your contentment. This was the secret Paul spoke about in the fourth chapter of Philippians when he said:

But I rejoiced in the Lord greatly, that now at last you have revived your concern for me; indeed, you were concerned before, but you lacked opportunity. Not that I speak from want, for I have learned to be content in whatever circumstances I am. I know how to get along with humble means, and I also know how to live in prosperity; in any and every circumstance I have learned the secret of being filled and going hungry, both of having abundance and suffering need. I can do all things through Him who strengthens me. (Phil. 4:10–13 NASB)

In the end, *Praying for Your Elephant* is about making the pursuit of knowing Jesus your greatest dream. For when it comes to the factory of dreams, nothing can compare with the greatest dream ever dreamed: that God Himself would come and make you His dwelling through the shed blood and resurrection of His Son, Jesus Christ.

It is only when our other dreams are purified through the filter of the cross that they will give us any lasting satisfaction and have eternal significance.

Here's the rub. That type of perspective and life takes faith, and faith is not cheap. Faith is forged in the valley of doubt. In fact, faith cannot exist without doubt. If it could, it would not be called faith; it would be called foregone conclusion. Faith is that substance that overcomes doubt. Faith has no victory unless it overcomes our doubts.

To be sure, by the time Susan Boyle sang the final note that night, her life had radically changed. She had instantly become more popular than Elaine Paige. The world was her oyster; her elephant had come home.

But as Boyle found out shortly after her personal victory, realized dreams can be just as dicey as those not met. Within two months of her dream-fulfilling moment, she found herself sitting in a psychiatric hospital suffering from exhaustion and trying to put the pieces back together.[2]

With that said, I want you to stop and think about the elephants you have been praying for since you were a kid, the ones you might actively be pursuing, the ones you might currently be living, and perhaps even the ones that somehow got lost along the way.

Now take your sacred dreams, place them on the altar of God, and sacrifice them. Stick a dagger in their hearts and receive the peace that comes from letting go. It is only when your dreams have been put to death that God can get to the business of resurrecting them in the way that He sees most fit. Is this not the model of the patriarch of our faith? We read in the book of Genesis, "After all this, God tested Abraham. God said, 'Abraham!' 'Yes?' answered Abraham. 'I'm listening.' He said, 'Take your dear son Isaac whom you love and go to the land of Moriah. Sacrifice him there as a burnt offering on one of the mountains that I'll point out to you'" (Gen. 22:1–2 MSG).

Unlike us, Abraham had a face-to-face encounter and conversation with God in which he was given a direct promise. The problem for Abraham and his wife Sarah was the promise had become more important than the promiser. Abraham and his wife had spent years chasing a dream that God had already guaranteed. And then, "after all this," Abraham finally got it right. He stopped chasing his dreams and started chasing God, realizing that if you are a child of God, you never need to chase your dreams. Rather, as we chase after God, our dreams will turn on their heels and chase after us.

Again, the concept of chasing dreams is more American than biblical. In the biblical paradigm, God is and always has been the pursuer. He has always been in the business of chasing us down and bringing our dreams to us. Jesus is enough. The book of Romans says, "For when we were yet without strength, in due time Christ died for the ungodly" (Rom. 5:6 KJV).

You see, when it comes to dreams and elephants, there are none greater or as grand as the God of the universe sending His only Son that He might not only make us His temple but commit to spending eternity with us. It is a dream He intends to fulfill. The third chapter of 1 Corinthians says, "Do you not know that you are a temple of God and that the Spirit of God dwells in you?" (1 Cor. 3:16 NASB). And then the book of Philippians says, "But our citizenship is in heaven, from which we also eagerly wait for a Savior, the Lord Jesus Christ. He will transform the body of our humble condition into the likeness of His glorious body, by the power that enables Him to subject everything to Himself" (Phil. 3:20–21 HCSB).

As I wrote earlier and must repeat at the expense of redundancy, when we understand that the only elephant that matters has already been realized by the gift of salvation in Jesus Christ, then we can start praying for those other elephants in our lives within their proper place and with reckless abandon.

Eugene Peterson's *The Message* gets right to the heart of this concept in his rendering of Christ's words on dream fulfillment from the Sermon on the Mount:

If God gives such attention to the appearance of wildflowers—most of which are never even seen—don't you think he'll attend to you, take pride in you, do his best for you? What I'm trying to do here is to get you to relax, to not be so preoccupied with *getting*, so you can respond to God's *giving*. People who don't know God and the way he works fuss over these things, but you know both God and how he works. Steep your life in God-reality, God-initiative, God-provisions. Don't worry about missing out. You'll find all your everyday human concerns will be met. (Matt. 6:30–33 MSG)

When we elevate God to His rightful place and put our elephants in theirs, our intended future will come and lie at our feet. Again, you do not need to chase the dreams God has for you. Only when they are sacrificed to Him do they hold the possibility of being resurrected. And this is the thing about God's dreams for you. You can't outrun them. They will pursue you with an unmatched and relentless force. When God is on the throne of your life and you are submitted to Him, your dreams, even your elephants, will chase you down and stampede your life. It is only then that you will find contentment.

The following story came to me last summer during a season of dryness in prayer. It was unique in that it came all at once as a full thought rather than as a progressive thought. I have never experienced this before or since. At the time I had no idea what its purpose might be, but I felt impressed to write it down. After sharing it with many friends and seeing its ability to bring peace to their elephant dreams and pursuits, I decided to add it here. I feel it has a profound ability to unpack the spirit and message of this chapter. I pray it blesses you.

The Fable of the Witch King and the Little Girl
A Modern Fable on Contentment and Purpose

Long ago, there lived the Witch King with the power to grant wishes. The only thing the Witch King would ask in return was a small piece of your soul for the privilege of being granted each wish. The wish could be as big as you wanted, but the price of the wish would remain the same. A small portion of your soul must be given to the Witch King, hardly enough to ever be noticed.

People came from near and far to request wishes from the Witch King. Some wanted to be made well, others desired fame and fortune. Many sought after position and power or even to be made beautiful. Barren women asked for children; men wanted enchanting wives.

Soon the power of the Witch King who granted wishes was known throughout the entire land. It seemed that none were immune to the desire to have what they wanted now. Happiness and fulfillment were only a wish away. And with the price of each wish costing so little, people were willing to wish again and again without a second thought. And who could blame them? A minute part of your soul for the ability to have the future of your desire now was a small price to pay.

What the people did not know was that the Witch King had hidden a small curse inside of every wish. The granting of the wish would fulfill them for a time, but eventually that fulfillment would fade and the wisher would be left with an even deeper desire than before.

The men who had been granted wives would long for the wives they had been given to be different. Those who had asked for wealth desired freedom from the management of all their treasures. Women who had requested beauty wanted someone who would love them for who they truly were and not for their beauty alone.

So the people would return over and over again to the Witch King, once again seeking fulfillment and happiness. Each time the Witch King would grant their wishes but also extract another little bit of their souls. In this way the Witch King slowly began to purchase the souls of all who lived in the kingdom.

Quickly, the people of the realm were enslaved to the curse of "the Wish." The more they wished, the more they desired another wish to fulfill all the voids that the previous wish had created. With each new wish their souls were becoming empty and along with it their lives in the constant search for fulfillment. The power and curse of the wish had stolen all satisfaction with life as they knew it. The beauty and contentment of "now" had been traded for the allure of a better "then."

One day the Witch King was wandering throughout the land looking for someone to destroy when he came upon a little girl playing in a field. The Witch King sat and watched the girl as she played among the golden sunflowers, chasing butterflies as they fluttered around her head.

As she ran, the Witch King noticed the little girl had a limp. One leg had been formed a few inches shorter than the other. Occasionally the little girl would fall while chasing the butterflies, her leg limiting her ability to capture the beautiful insects.

Seeing his opportunity, the Witch King approached the little girl. "What beautiful butterflies," he said. "Oh yes," said the little girl. "How I love chasing them." "But would you not like to catch one?" asked the Witch King. "If one were to ever come to me, I would love to hold it," said the girl. The Witch King, hungry for souls, responded, "What if I could grant you a wish that would give you all of the butterflies you ever wanted? You would never need to chase butterflies again. Would that not be what you most desire?" The girl stopped and thought. Then she said, "But if you did that, I would not need to chase butterflies, and oh, how I love chasing butterflies."

Frustrated, the Witch King tried to convince the little girl that capturing butterflies was the object of chasing them, to which the girl responded, "If I ever did catch a butterfly, I would only hold it lightly and for a moment before I let it go; for I do not believe that butterflies are meant to be kept, but rather free. Does not a caged butterfly lose some of its beauty?" she asked. By now, the Witch King was becoming angry. If the little girl would not wish for a world of butterflies, then he would offer her something she would surely want. Cruelly, the Witch King said, "And why do you run so slowly, little girl? Do you not wish to be like all the other girls? Would you not rather be normal?"

"What is normal?" asked the little girl.

"Normal is when you are like everyone else," replied the Witch King. Here again the little girl paused for a long time. Finally, looking up at the Witch King, she said, "I do not want that wish either. I think I would much rather be me than be whatever normal is."

The Witch King looked as if a blade had pierced him. A visible pain shone on his face, and if one were to look upon him, they would have noticed he had slightly shrunk with the girl's words. By now the girl no longer paid attention to the Witch King but rather ran about chasing butterflies in the warm sun. This enraged the Witch King and caused a lust for souls within him that he had never experienced before. He was willing to give anything if the little girl would make just one small wish. "Little girl," he said. "I beg your pardon, but please let me ask you just one more question. What would you say if I told you that I could grant you any wish you ever wanted, even if it were to rule all of the kingdoms in the world?"

The little girl stopped chasing her butterflies and was again silent for a long time. Then with the purest of intention, she looked upon the Witch King and said, "Kind sir, I have tried and tried to think and think for a wish I deeply desired and to play this game with you, but if I could have a wish, I would wish for what I already have and that is not really a wish at all."

With that the Witch King began to shrink and writhe in pain, screaming until he eventually vanished. The spell had been broken, the curse undone, for the Witch King could not exist in the presence of perfect contentment. Just then a butterfly landed in the palm of the little girl's hand. For a moment it sat batting its wings in her open hand. Then it flew away again. As it flew away, the little girl began again to run enraptured in the pleasure of just chasing butterflies.

CHAPTER 11

THE ELEPHANT GRAVEYARD

Love consists not in feeling great things, but in having
great detachment and in suffering for the Beloved.
—Saint John of the Cross

Legend suggests that when elephants instinctively know their time on this earth is coming to an end, they begin their final migration to a place known as an elephant's graveyard. Here, among the dry bones, the elephants lie down, breathe their last breaths, and die.

Unlike when these elephants pass away, the elephants in our lives that seem to die often continue to wander about in our souls, hearts, and minds, haunting us with thoughts of what could have been or what should now be. Here in the desolation of broken dreams, many believers have lost their way. When their elephant prayers went unanswered and seemed to die, their hope died with them. Unlike the elephants making their way to the graveyard, these people had no internal compass directing them where to go when their elephants died.

Here is where praying for an elephant in your life finds its danger. These are elephants after all and not mice. Anytime you are in the presence of elephants, one needs be careful, as elephants have been known to charge.

To pray boldly for anything that matters deeply to you puts you at risk, great risk. As a man I counseled once said, "I would rather not pray for something than be disappointed when it doesn't happen." And this is the problem with praying for elephants at all. To hope, imagine, and dream is human, but none of these commodities can exist without risk. Yes, Jesus implored us to boldly ask for anything in His name. He promised that He would give us what we asked for. But there is one caveat to His promise. What we pray for needs to walk the razor's edge of God's intent and best wisdom.

And this is the thing with God. Like elephants that will not supersede their instincts for the sake of personal desire, God will not disregard what is best for the sake of your wants.

When God gave me my elephant that hot and sticky night in Thailand, I understood it as a confirmation to me that leaving my youth group in Newport Beach was the right thing to do. It also opened the door for what at that time was the biggest elephant hope and dream of my life: the opportunity to move to and minister in Australia.

Within thirty-six months I was sitting on the beaches of the Gold Coast of Australia having moved my family from California and taken a job with Christian Surfers, a parachurch ministry that reaches out to people steeped in beach culture. With the majority of

Australia's population living within a couple of hours' drive of the ocean, this was a fertile ground for ministry.

I had originally visited Australia in 1989 as a traveling surfer running from God. I fell in love with the country, its culture, its ethos, and its people. Over the few months I sojourned in Oz and later Indonesia, God started the massive work of calling me home. It's a story too long to tell for this book, but even in the midst of running from God, He was laying the groundwork for me to return to Australia years later. This time it would be on His terms.

Fast-forward to 2005 and my elephant could not have been doing better. It was fat and happy; life and ministry were thriving. People were making decisions for Christ, and we were living and surfing on one of the best right-hand point breaks in the world. The coffee was good and the sand warm. I was literally living smack-dab in the middle of my dream. Then my elephant died.

JOSEPH, GOD'S DREAMER

Perhaps no one in the Bible understood the death and resurrection of dreams better than Joseph did. The problem for Joseph was that the resurrected version of his dream didn't much resemble the one he had originally desired. Perhaps you know what I mean.

Scripture paints a picture of Joseph as God's dreamer who at seventeen years of age dreamed a dream that would shake the entire world. Its cataclysmic effects still ripple today. His story is told in Genesis:

> Joseph had a dream. When he told it to his brothers,
> they hated him even more. He said, "Listen to this

dream I had. We were all out in the field gathering bundles of wheat. All of a sudden my bundle stood straight up and your bundles circled around it and bowed down to mine."

His brothers said, "So! You're going to rule us? You're going to boss us around?" And they hated him more than ever because of his dreams and the way he talked.

He had another dream and told this one also to his brothers: "I dreamed another dream—the sun and moon and eleven stars bowed down to me!"

When he told it to his father and brothers, his father reprimanded him: "What's with all this dreaming? Am I and your mother and your brothers all supposed to bow down to you?" Now his brothers were really jealous; but his father brooded over the whole business. (Gen. 37:5–11 MSG)

THE DREAM SHEPHERD

Besides being a dreamer, Joseph was also a boy of the pasture who knew how to herd sheep; but he had no clue how to shepherd his dreams. It is one thing to dream and pray for elephants, but it is another to have the ability to shepherd them into existence.

Before Joseph's head hit the pillow the night of his first dream, he had already been set up for failure by a doting father who cared more about appeasing his own emotions than providing a safe place for his son to blossom into his calling and into his dreams.

Instead of crafting a son of wisdom and restraint, he created an entitled, arrogant, self-absorbed dream worshipper. As we learned in the last chapter, God will not stand for our dreams to be worshipped above Him.

Not long after, when Joseph's dreams were in the bottom of a pit, the young man began the long journey to dream fulfillment. It was a hard road and one that took him places that he would rather not have gone. The book of Genesis tells us, "When Joseph reached his brothers, they ripped off the fancy coat he was wearing, grabbed him, and threw him into a cistern. The cistern was dry; there wasn't any water in it" (Gen. 37:23–24 MSG). To put it bluntly, Joseph's dreams ended up in a pit.

Here again we come face-to-face with one of the risks inherent to praying for elephants. Sometimes our elephants take us where we would rather not go. **Like Christ's dream to see His children saved from hellfire, oftentimes our dreams must first endure a cross before they are fulfilled.** And it is here, where our greatest prayers seem more fantasy than possibility, that God gets about the work of changing us and our dreams into something He can use for His glory.

Fast-forward a couple of decades in Joseph's life. By the time his dreams finally came to fruition, his life had changed. Like Dorothy in Oz, Joseph wasn't in Kansas anymore. And the dream Joseph was living looked strikingly different from the one he had imagined. At times it had been a nightmare. Now, years later and dressed in the garb and face paint common to Egyptian aristocracy, Joseph had become a different man, perhaps closer to a pharaoh than an Israelite. His vision quest had turned him into someone different from who he had previously been and perhaps never wanted to be.

Not only had Joseph been thrown into a pit, but instead of riding on a superhighway to dream fulfillment, Joseph had taken the long way around to the land of answered prayers and shattered dreams. It was a journey that had made him a slave, a household servant, a prisoner, and finally the right-hand man to the ruler himself. In the end, we can't help but wonder if as Joseph watched his brothers bow low before him, he thought about whether the struggle to achieve his dream had been worth it. Maybe Kansas wasn't such a bad place after all.

THE DAY MY ELEPHANT DIED

Like the story of Joseph, I have seen hundreds of people's dreams come true. And like Joseph, I have watched as many of them also lost everything in the process.

On the day my elephant died in Australia, I was faced with a similar challenge. After almost a year of living on the other side of the earth, my wife, Karie, came to me and said, "I want you to know that you are the only man for me. I will never seek another. There is no plan B. I'm just not sure I can live with you right now. I want to go home."

As my Australian elephant lay there writhing in pain, I was faced with a decision. I could call it quits then and there or try to resuscitate my elephant, giving it CPR and convincing my wife that she was wrong, and then forge on with a stiff upper lip. After all, two weeks prior we had hosted one of the largest Christian surfers events the Gold Coast had ever seen. God was on the move, and there were plenty of good reasons and manipulative tools I had learned over the years to convince my wife that what she was feeling was not God's will. And I might have convinced her—for a while.

But there was another option, a more painful solution. It was to drag my beloved elephant out back behind the spiritual shed, load the blunderbuss, say a prayer, and put it out of its misery. And that is what I did. After seeking God and the wise counsel of mentors, I called the leaders of Christian Surfers Australia and told them we were going home. It was a decision, to their credit, they fully agreed with. These were men who cared more about the people of the ministry than the ministry. To them I am forever grateful.

It's now a decade later, and looking back, it all makes sense. For one thing, the elephant I so desired was more mine than it was ours as a couple. Marriage struggles when vision is unequally yoked. Today I want nothing to do with elephants that my wife will not pray for with me.

Within three months of coming home, God moved dramatically. He provided a great job, and our marriage had been resurrected from the ashes. Hope reigned again, but not without some regret and longing for my lost elephant. And this is what Jesus does. He is in the business of restoration and redemption. Yes, I lost an elephant, but Karie and I found another one—each other.

If there is one thing I have learned about elephants, it is this: It's not about the elephant. It never has been. It's about Jesus and your relationship with Him. You are Christ's beloved, the apple of

His eye, and the focus of His intent. It is in chasing and riding the elephants of our lives that God continues the work of creating you in the image of who you truly are meant to be.

THE BACK SIDE OF AN ELEPHANT AND SCRIPTURAL BAND-AIDS

People say hindsight is twenty-twenty. This is definitely true. Looking back, I realize that it took a dead elephant to save my marriage, and I am thankful for that, but it still did not make grieving for my elephant any less painful. I was angry, embarrassed, and depressed. None of it made sense. Why would God let me have what I wanted only to rip it from my grasp less than a year later?

Here we come to the crux of life after elephants. How do you live on the back side of your dreams? What do you do when you are faced with the back side of an elephant? It's not a pretty sight.

As a writer, I realize that I need to tread lightly here. Many of you have faced a loss of much greater significance than having to move back to Southern California. One thing I don't want to do is give scriptural Christianese Band-Aids to people who have lost limbs. God's Word is effective and powerful for all situations, but I have found that Scripture does not fix everything in the moment. Some of the promises of Scripture God has given me made no sense in the moment they were given. They would take years and decades to play out and to find true meaning in my life. Perhaps you already understand that.

Paul talked about life on the back side of an elephant in his letter of joy to the Philippians. Here Paul wrote of a "secret" that he had discovered when it came to living in joyful contentment in all situations. This secret is the key to being able to carry on after the loss of an elephant. He said, "I know what it is to be in need, and I know what it is to have plenty. I have learned the secret of being content in any and every situation, whether well fed or hungry, whether living in plenty or in want. I can do all this through him who gives me strength" (Phil. 4:12–13).

Thankfully in this case, Paul was not very good at keeping secrets, and he let the elephant out of the bag in verse 13.

Paul's secret was Jesus.

Paul had a deep and unending hope and confidence in a God who was greater than any situation. Jesus was a situational game changer for Paul. When there is nothing in the world you want more than Jesus, nothing in the world really matters, even elephants.

FORGIVING GOD

Here again, we are faced with a scriptural truth that on the surface makes a lot of sense. The problem is that this understanding might take a lifetime to attain. Perhaps it will even mean having to forgive God.

This is what a good friend of mine told me recently. Ten years ago, after thirty years of frustration and dead ends here in San Diego, she had packed up and moved to New York City. She told me how this was supposed to be the move that changed everything. And for the first five years, it seemed like it had. Each time she visited back home, she would keep me updated on all the happenings back east. Her new job came with an amazing apartment next to Central Park, and she had become part of an exciting church plant. There were even a few boyfriends who were marriage material.

But as the seasons turned into years and years turned into a decade, things had not really changed that much after all. The geography was different and the faces new, but she was still battling some of the same emotional and spiritual issues she had faced when she was stuck here in San Diego, far from the bright lights and big city. Now as we talked in the church courtyard, there was an authentic realness I had never seen in her before. The job had ended, the apartment was no more, and those candidates for betrothal had found other fantastic wives. **At forty-four years of age she told me she found herself in the place of having to ask the Holy Spirit to help her forgive God.**

Forgiving God is something counterintuitive to everything I ever learned in seminary and Bible college. Of course we know that God never does anything in His perfection that would need to be forgiven, but as frail human beings with limited understandings, we can still become trapped in feelings of distrust or anger with God. On the campuses of spiritual answers and biblical truth, tensions are resolved, questions sorted out, and grades given. Many of life's deepest problems are given bumper-sticker answers.

What I have learned on the playing field of ministry and far from the classrooms of academia is that things are a lot different in real life than in the lecture hall.

In the froth and bubble of life's realities, not every kid who gets cancer lives. Not every couple who wants desperately to be parents has children. And not every woman who moves to New York City is satisfied from the bite she has taken from the Big Apple.

DAVID AND JOB

In trying to think of scriptural examples of people who have wrestled with anger, disappointment, and forgiveness of God, my mind immediately went to David and Job.

In David's case, God had actually afflicted his first son by Bathsheba with a disease that would take his life. David had sinned greatly against God, but was taking the life of the baby really God's best way of doing things? The story is told in 2 Samuel:

> After Nathan went home, GOD afflicted the child that Uriah's wife bore to David, and he came down sick. David prayed desperately to God for the little boy. He fasted, wouldn't go out, and slept on the floor. The elders in his family came in and tried to get him off the floor, but he wouldn't budge. Nor could they get him to eat anything. On the seventh day the child died. David's servants were afraid to tell him. They said, "What do we do now? While the child was living he wouldn't listen to a word we said. Now, with the child dead, if we speak to him there's no telling what he'll do."
> (2 Sam. 12:15–18 MSG)

Then there was Job. God had allowed Satan to have his way with him. He had removed the veil of protection over Job. And God did it all because the Devil dared him to do so after God had suggested Job as a possible candidate for affliction. Really, God?

GOD said to Satan, "Have you noticed my friend Job? There's no one quite like him—honest and true to his word, totally devoted to God and hating evil."

Satan retorted, "So do you think Job does all that out of the sheer goodness of his heart? Why, no one ever had it so good! You pamper him like a pet, make sure nothing bad ever happens to him or his family or his possessions, bless everything he does—he can't lose!

"But what do you think would happen if you reached down and took away everything that is his? He'd curse you right to your face, that's what."

GOD replied, "We'll see. Go ahead—do what you want with all that is his. Just don't hurt *him*." Then Satan left the presence of GOD. (Job 1:8–12 MSG)

While these things make no sense to me and perhaps never will, what does resonate is the way these biblical heroes dealt with their anger and disappointment with God.

For instance, when David heard that the boy had died, he got up, got ready, and did the one thing he knew. It is the one thing he is most known for. He went to the house of God and worshipped.

Then David got up from the ground. After he had washed, put on lotions and changed his clothes, he went into the house of the LORD and worshiped.

Then he went to his own house, and at his request they served him food, and he ate.

His attendants asked him, "Why are you acting this way? While the child was alive, you fasted and wept, but now that the child is dead, you get up and eat!"

He answered, "While the child was still alive, I fasted and wept. I thought, 'Who knows? The LORD may be gracious to me and let the child live.' But now that he is dead, why should I go on fasting? Can I bring him back again? I will go to him, but he will not return to me." (2 Sam. 12:20–23)

Let's look at Job's response. After coming to the end of himself, sitting in his extreme poverty, his cursed flesh unrecognizable to even his closest friends, Job made a statement that would make angels sit up and take note. He said, "Though he slay me, yet will I trust in him" (Job 13:15 KJV).

I believe this statement by Job contains perhaps the greatest words ever spoken by a human being other than the direct confession of Christ Jesus as Lord. It is a statement that strikes to the heart of ultimate discipleship. They are words that I have sought to anchor my life to. They are the words of people who have come to the end of self and found God.

This is what dead elephants tend to do. They lead us to the end of ourselves. They remind us of our desperation, and they leave us with a choice. Will we "curse God and die" as was the advice of Job's wife, or will we realize like David and Job that when there is nowhere left to go, we should seek God in prayer? Abraham Lincoln expressed the desperation of coming to the end of himself in this way: "I have been driven many times upon my knees by the overwhelming conviction that I had nowhere else to go. My own wisdom and that of all about me seemed insufficient for that day."[1]

LIFE AFTER ELEPHANTS

Last summer after my brother-in-law took his life, I received an email from Karie's mom, Pat. I call her my other mom. While life has many possible and difficult roads we can travel, perhaps none can compare to the loss of a child. The fact that God chose this route with His own Son to show His love for us perhaps validates this. In the book of John we read, "For God so loved the world that he gave his one and only Son, that whoever believes in him shall not perish but have eternal life" (John 3:16).

I debated whether to share this sacred email with the world. After speaking with Pat and getting her blessing, I decided to include it. I did it for a few reasons. The first is that I needed someone who has more authority on grief, loss, and life after elephants than I have to speak to the sacredness of this topic. What Pat wrote describes God's goodness in living life after elephants. It is far better than anything I could craft.

Next, I wanted to give hope to many of you who, like Joseph, are dealing with circumstances in your life that turned out differently than you expected. Perhaps this letter should be addressed to "Those Currently Living in Egypt." Know that I pray for you.

But perhaps the greatest reason I decided to include Pat's letter about Devin in *Praying for Your Elephant* is that by doing so I am allowing God to further the calling of ministry that many of us who knew Devin best believed he had on his life.

What has been so encouraging is how God has continued to further and confirm that calling even after his death. While I don't have the space to recount all the amazing ways God has used Devin after his death to minister, I will say that it already seems that they will surpass what he did while alive and with us.

In the end, what we have learned as a family is that you can't kill an elephant if it was truly God's elephant to begin with. Yes, Devin took his life, but that did not in any way inhibit God's plans to use him as He sees fit. The following email is part of God's fulfillment of Devin's calling. It is not the way we wanted to see Devin minister, but then again, when were we ever encouraged to lean on our own understanding of how things should be?

We lost our son June 23. His suicide was a result of years of living with bipolar disorder and finally a drug overdose. We had him in our lives for thirty-six years. These were not always peaceful years, but they were filled with a lot of love.

Devin was a much prayed-for child. When he was young I prayed most often for salvation and safety. He gave his life to Jesus at four years of age. As for safety, this would be a prayer I would continue to pray for the remainder of his life. During his younger years he was very accident-prone, thus I often asked for physical safety as well as spiritual safety. God consistently answered this prayer throughout Devin's life, first with trips and falls (skateboarding was his favorite sport, then snowboarding) and then later in his life when he turned to drugs as a form of self-medication.

Unbeknownst to his parents, he started using alcohol and marijuana in jr. high and high school to deal with the depression that would plague him all of his life. Once I knew of his drug use I added a prayer that the Lord would allow him to always be caught or discovered in his drug use. I do not know whether or not it was a result of my prayers, but he first ended up in jail in his early twenties and then again in his mid-twenties. Once again the Lord answered my prayers for protection as many times the jails became dangerous and Devin would be moved or relocated just before a riot or other violence, sometimes within hours of the event.

He was near death more times than I probably am aware of throughout those years but the Lord allowed him to survive and stay with us. During those years I had a picture of him by my bed from when he was five and I daily asked the Lord to return to me the child who had a strong pure faith in Jesus. Dev once asked me why I had that picture by my bed and I explained to him my daily prayer.

Over the years I prayed for his education, jobs, a healing of his relationship with his dad, a relationship with his own young son, a God-fearing woman to become his wife and an increasing faith that would allow him to minister for God. And always for protection and a return to that faith he had as a child.

God blessed us with six plus years of a drug-free relationship with Devin towards the end of his life. He finished his bachelor's degree in Social Services and began working on his master's degree. He was working full-time in a job he felt he was good at, helping others that had walked the same path he had. He rebuilt a relationship with his dad, he started to reconnect with his son and three months before his death he married. Looking back, those were really good years filled with so many blessings and answers to prayer.

There were over two hundred and fifty people at his memorial service, most of whom I had never met. After his death God gave us the precious gift of allowing us to see how dramatically Devin touched so many lives. All those years that I had been praying for God to prepare him for His use, God was already using him. His impact on so many lives just blew me away. He encouraged and uplifted so many people during his life. Less than a month after Dev's death I began to pray that his death would produce fruit. Devin's wife recommitted her life to Jesus and started a weekly Bible study, several of his closest friends are more active in seeking the Lord, and a neighbor and I have started praying each Wednesday for the children in our neighborhood.

As I write this on the day after Thanksgiving, I have to say I am so thankful that God has answered so many of this mother's prayers for her son. Towards the end of Devin's life I was desperately praying that he would find peace and strength in the Lord once again. The Lord answered that prayer choosing to take my son home—not the outcome I had hoped for, but I have learned that God's way is always more perfect than mine. I no longer have to pray for my son as I know he is with his Savior, so I now continue to pray for my daughter, son-in-love, granddaughters, grandson, and husband knowing that God does hear and answer the prayers of His beloved children.

*Trust in the LORD with all your heart
And do not lean on your own understanding.
In all your ways acknowledge Him,
And He will make your paths straight. (Prov. 3:5–6 NASB)*

CONCLUSION
THE QUEST

CHAPTER 12

LAND GRAB

We shall not cease from exploration, and the end of
all our exploring will be to arrive where we started
and know the place for the first time.

—T. S. Eliot

Be strong and courageous, because you will lead these people
to inherit the land I swore to their ancestors to give them.

—Joshua 1:6

Perhaps few things ignite the human spirit like quest. For in quest we find all the glorious plotlines available to us on this grand odyssey called life. Quest encapsulates not only hope and high adventure but the opportunity to face our giants, navigate life's comedy and tragedy, and book return passage on a voyage to personal rebirth and renewal. It is here on the frontier of exploration's hope that we look out at what is beyond us and ask the immortal question—what if?

"What if" is the segue between what currently is and what might be. "What if" is a question that can hold as much hope as it does fear. "What if" asks questions such as: What if you were to cash it all in and pursue that thing you know you were created for? What if you asked her to be your wife? What if you went to Cambodia to work with children sold into sex trafficking?

Of course, there are all those other "what ifs" that have to do with the possible tragic things that could happen to us like, what if I get a terminal illness? While these "what ifs" are valid, they have no purpose in today's conversation. Today we speak only of hope. As it says in Romans, "Hope does not disappoint, because the love of God has been poured out within our hearts through the Holy Spirit who was given to us" (Rom. 5:5 NASB).

Perhaps nothing sets the "what ifs" of your life into motion like the discipline of prayer. Prayer, combined with wise and determined action in the direction of those petitions, acts like a jackhammer loosening the sediment of God's intention and setting it free.

FAR AND AWAY

Recently my wife and I watched a movie that focused on the hopeful "what ifs" of two Irish expatriates to America near the turn of the twentieth century. In *Far and Away*, Tom Cruise and Nicole Kidman play two Irish immigrants to America. Much of the tension of the movie comes from the relationship of these two main characters' diametrically opposed social classes and growing love for each other. Cruise's character, Joseph Donnelly, is a poor farmer and bare-knuckles brawler who dreams of coming to the land of answered dreams and starting afresh with a plot of fertile soil to call his own. For Kidman, who plays Shannon Christie, the search is less about land and more about identity. As a child of Irish aristocracy, her character longs to find herself far from the confines of upper-class etiquette.

I'm not going to lie. I love this movie. I had forgotten how much. Perhaps what I like most is the characters' authentic and hard-fought struggle to answer their own personal "what ifs."

The film climaxes during the Oklahoma Land Run of 1893, an actual historic event where over 100,000 settlers raced from a starting line at noon on September 16 to stake a claim to one of thousands of free parcels available on a first-come, first-served basis. The 6.5 million acres available for the taking represented the largest land grab of its kind in US history. I'll let you watch the film to see what happens to Joseph, Shannon, and their quest to answer the "what ifs" of their lives. Today let's examine yours.

Like Joseph and Shannon, you, too, have "what ifs." Many of these would be situational game changers if they came about. Like the starting line from which the settlers raced for their dreams in 1893, prayer is the starting line of your life and acts as a land grab into your future. The question is, will you prayerfully stake your claim to it?

With that said, I want to circle back to the purpose of this book. If you have not sorted it out yet, the purpose of this work is to challenge you to ask anything of Christ in prayer. Throughout the book we have processed many thoughts on prayer, but at the heart of it all is a simple premise. Will you ask for anything in Jesus's name? Are you willing to overcome any mountain that stands in your way?

CASTING MOUNTAINS

In the eleventh chapter of Mark, Jesus implored believers with the challenge to cast mountains into the sea. Jesus said, "Truly I say to you, whoever says to this mountain, 'Be taken up and cast into the sea,' and does not doubt in his heart, but believes that what he says is going to happen, it will be granted him" (Mark 11:23 NASB).

Admittedly, the verse is set in the context of big faith, and this is a stumbling block for many people. We often feel that in verses like these Jesus sets the bar so high we might as well not even jump. And so the mountains in our lives never get moved.

The place to start when moving mountains is to speak to the mountain. Because so many people feel that they lack the faith to see mountains moved, they never speak to mountains in the first place. Speaking to mountains is the first step in seeing them moved. If you never speak to a mountain, it will never be moved.

Think about the man with the demon-possessed son. His mountain was the healing of his son. His quest to see his boy healed did not start with faith but rather the willingness to bring his son to Jesus, the true mountain, and ask for help:

> "How long has this been happening to him?" Jesus asked his father.
>
> "From childhood," he said. "And many times it has thrown him into fire or water to destroy him. But if You can do anything, have compassion on us and help us."

> Then Jesus said to him, "'If You can'?
> Everything is possible to the one who believes."
> Immediately the father of the boy cried out,
> "I do believe! Help my unbelief." (Mark 9:21–24
> HCSB)

When approaching this passage, we need to consider the following. The man who brought his son to Jesus did not have the faith to see the boy healed. Scripture makes this clear. He had to source the faith to believe from Jesus. This is something we must realize about faith and prayer. The faith to move mountains is not something we possess on our own like a pocket watch or some other treasure. Rather, faith is a gift given to us by God. And God is in the business of giving this gift of faith away for free to those who ask. The book of Romans says, "For through the grace given to me I say to everyone among you not to think more highly of himself than he ought to think; but to think so as to have sound judgment, as God has allotted to each a measure of faith" (Rom. 12:3 NASB).

I want to encourage you not to fail in speaking to mountains because of a perceived lack of faith. Rather, speak to God first for the faith to believe, and then stand in that faith and speak to your mountain.

GRACE

The need for faith was just one of the conditions that Jesus mentioned to see the boy in Mark 9 released from the evil spirit's grasp.

If you were to read through the rest of the story, you would see that Jesus set forth another stipulation to see the boy healed. In the end this requirement was also left unfulfilled. Yet, still the boy was healed.

Christ told His disciples that the answer to this particular request would only come through the means of prayer and fasting. (See Mark 9:29 KJV.) Unless they called an immediate fast that is not mentioned in the story, we know this condition was not met.

So the questions are: Why was the boy healed if the faith was lacking and prayer and fasting were not present? Why was this mountain thrown into the sea if those asking for it to be moved were so inadequate not only in preparation (prayer and fasting) but also in the faith needed to see their petition granted?

The answer is simple. Grace.

Grace is always the answer to effectual prayer.

Answered prayer is not about spiritual perfection or the ability to follow a set of rules that appease God. If it were, prayer would become law. Jesus wants us to journey with Him in the growing of our faith through prayer. He wants us to experience and explore what happens when we use spiritual disciplines like fasting and prayer. But here again, Christ implores us to do these things because He knows they increase opportunity for relationship with Him. When we fail in these pursuits, as we regularly will, Jesus is still often willing to grant our requests because of His great compassion and mercy.

What this story shows us is that those with imperfect faith can still see mountains moved in their lives simply because of grace.

USING A MOUNTAIN TO MOVE MOUNTAINS

There is another thing about moving mountains that you must know. The best way to move a mountain is with a mountain. That mountain is God. When we ascend the mountain of God in prayer, we realize that every other mountain in our lives, even the ones that look like Mount Everest, are really molehills that pale in comparison to the greatness, power, and grandeur that is the mountain of God. (See Isa. 2.) When we speak to mountains from the mountain who is God, those other mountains quake and melt before us. The book of Judges says, "The mountains quaked at the presence of the LORD, this Sinai, at the presence of the LORD, the God of Israel" (Judg. 5:5 NASB). Then we read in the book of Isaiah, "Even those I will bring to My holy mountain and make them joyful in My house of prayer. Their burnt offerings and their sacrifices will be acceptable on My altar; for My house will be called a house of prayer for all the peoples" (Isa. 56:7 NASB).

As you look at the mountains that stand before you, know that it is grace that will move them, not some perfection of function or perfection of faith on your part. Know also that the only way to move these mountains is to approach the mountain of God in prayer. This was the secret of the father seeking deliverance for his son. This should be your secret too.

LAND GRABBING

Here again we stand with our toes in the river of prayer's intention; for prayer's mission is not only to open your eyes to all the eternal possibilities that lie before you but also to cut a deep gorge into their fulfillment. (See Josh. 3:13.)

Think again about Joseph and Shannon laying claim to their future. Prayer is our guide in the exploration and quest of this life. Without prayer, much of the inheritance God has for you in this life will be left unexplored, unconquered, and dispossessed. Every day we fail to allow prayer a central place in our lives is a day we miss something God has intended for us.

My wife recently shared something she learned in a Beth Moore Bible study about possessing the things in our lives God has called us to. Moore said that anything you leave unclaimed in your life will be possessed by the Enemy. I would add that if it were not possessed by the Enemy, the other option would be that it would become a dry and waterless wasteland filled with jackals.

Like those early Oklahoma settlers standing in the hot sun with their feet on the starting line, your life and God's inheritance for it lie before you. Are you willing to plunge a claim deep into the heart of it through prayer?

This is where the spiritual land grab of our lives must begin. It begins in prayer. It begins by grabbing eternal territory first and believing it will lead to expansion of that which is located in the temporal now.

Here is where many believers go astray. They feel that the map to territory expansion begins in every direction under the sun except the one that matters—prayer. We are wired to trust our own instincts and follow our own ways. (See Isa. 48:17.) We believe too much in our own sense of direction and that apart from God we can create our own paths. (See Prov. 3:6.)

REMEMBER JABEZ

Perhaps you remember the Jabez craze that swept through the church years back. Whatever your thoughts on that phenomenon, there is one key understanding we can glean from this story. Jabez understood that the first step in territory expansion was in the direction of heaven and through prayer.

What Jabez knew was that prayer has the ability to exponentially expand your boundaries far beyond anything you can do in your own strength. Jabez took heavenly ground before he took earthly ground. The first book of Chronicles says, "Jabez called upon the God of Israel, saying, 'Oh that you would bless me and enlarge my border, and that your hand might be with me, and that you would keep me from harm so that it might not bring me pain!' And God granted what he asked" (1 Chron. 4:10 ESV).

This lesson from Jabez is one you need to firmly implant into your spiritual arsenal. Whether it be your marriage, friendships, work, health, finances, or relationship with your kids, the territory you are looking to increase must first be increased by prayerful exploration and possession.

At the risk of repeating myself, let me ask you this: Where do you start when it comes to the territory expansion of your life? How prone are you to attack the inheritance that lies before you in your own strength? Or do you instinctually turn to prayer?

THE REFLEX OF PRAYER

While prayer has many possible goals, I believe one of them should be allowing it to enter your subconscious—to become instinct. The speed and frequency at which you turn to prayer is something that can be developed. It takes no expertise to turn prayer from exercise into something second nature, perhaps even first nature. What it takes is commitment. Like our natural reflexes, prayer can also become reflexive.

As you know, a reflex is an involuntary and nearly instantaneous movement in response to a stimulus. The goal is to commit to regular and consistent prayer to the point that it becomes the first reflex to the stimuli of life.

While I still consider myself a complete novice in the eternal landscape that is prayer, I have noticed that prayer is finally becoming a reflex for me. Today I often become aware that I have been praying silently under my breath before it became a conscious thought. On occasion I will wake up praying and interceding for people in the middle of the night. Many nights I have awoken in tears and in deep intercession for people. And last week while in a movie, I found myself unintentionally praying over the safety of one of the characters.

While it is completely ridiculous to pray for a movie character, I left the theater feeling encouraged. What it showed me was that prayer was becoming my answer and starting place. Prayer has somehow commandeered my soul and thoughts beyond my conscious decision to engage in the pursuit. Let me again assure you that I am a complete novice in prayer. These things amaze and astound me when they happen. But that is the thing with prayer. If you commit to it in weakness and with determined resolve, it will commandeer your life. In this way then, prayer transitions from spiritual practice to spiritual piracy.

SPIRITUAL EXPATRIATES

There is one more thought that I want to pen before coming in for a landing on *Praying for Your Elephant*. It is the challenge to become a spiritual expatriate. Here is what I mean.

In his book *A Moveable Feast*, Ernest Hemingway told the story of American and British expatriates who throw off the confines of traditional living and head for the lights, cafés, and academia of Paris's Latin Quarter.

The book is semiautobiographical. Hemingway was an expatriate who moved to Paris in the 1920s. In France, he penned some of his finest work as an author while living among other expatriates, such as literary giants F. Scott Fitzgerald, Gertrude Stein, James Joyce, and Ezra Pound.

Perhaps few spiritual disciplines offer us the ability to expatriate from this world into the next like prayer. When we pray, we are making a conscious effort to allow a foreign culture to change our attitudes, thoughts, and perspectives. The more time you spend in God's presence through the rhythm of prayer, the more the cultural idiosyncrasies of that place will begin to shape you. Your anger will be changed to forgiveness, your despair to hope, your sorrow to joy, and so forth.

ONE FOOT IN ETERNITY AND ONE ON THIS EARTH

Prayer aids us in transferring our conscious citizenship from this world into the next. Prayer is a passport that allows us immigration into God's kingdom. Each time we pray, we embark on another sojourn to the place that will one day be our eternal home and in so doing better understand our lives in the present. Prayer, then, is transcendental. Prayer gives deeper understanding of your now, meaning it allows us to slip behind the veil of this temporal world and into the ethereal one where God our Father dwells. The writer of Hebrews alluded to this in his letter: "Let us then approach God's throne of grace with confidence, so that we may receive mercy and find grace to help us in our time of need" (Heb. 4:16).

What that verse is saying is that prayer allows us the ability to actually go before God's throne each time we pray. Please note that I am not suggesting we physically leave this world each time we pray. With that said, though, there is some biblical credibility for this possibility also. In the book of 2 Corinthians, Paul said, "I know a man in Christ who fourteen years ago—whether in the body I do not know, or out of the body I do not know, God knows—such a man was caught up to the third heaven" (2 Cor. 12:2 NASB).

What I am comfortable saying is that prayer allows us to be other-worldly. The more we pray and spend time before God's throne, the more our earthly identity will reflect our true and heavenly one and the more we will make decisions in alignment with God's governance rather than our own. And the more the kingdom of our personal lives will reflect that of God's. The book of Philippians talks about this repatriation this way: "But our citizenship is in heaven, and from it we await a Savior, the Lord Jesus Christ, who will transform our lowly body to be like his glorious body, by the power that enables him even to subject all things to himself" (Phil. 3:20–21 ESV).

Eventually, as Paul stated, we will take up permanent residency in our true country. Until then we are called to live in this world as if we are from that heavenly one. The problem is that it is hard to emulate a culture that you have never experienced or rarely see.

When we go to God in prayer, we spend time surveying the landscape of heaven. The kingdom of God on earth is made manifest when we allow the landscape of our lives to match the geography we explore in heaven through prayer.

IN CONCLUSION

It's now nearing two decades since Big Al and I prayed for that elephant together and about two thousand years since Jesus challenged His followers to pray for theirs. Today the challenge of Jesus to His followers remains the same. Will you ask for anything in His name?

Since taking this challenge by Jesus onboard as a life calling, I have seen horizons and vistas open up before me that I know I would have never seen or experienced without the power of simple asking prayer. The book you hold in your hands is just one example of this. I never asked to write a book about elephants, just to touch one.

And this is my hope for you. I am praying that you will experience the same. I am praying fervently for your elephants. I have asked God for one hundred million elephants for those who read this book and respond to its call to ask in prayer!

Yes, I know this seems like a ridiculous number of answers to ask God for, but I have asked for it nonetheless. My only fear is that I have perhaps requested too few. Maybe I should ask for twice as many. But whatever number I decide on, know that I am praying specifically for your elephants. I am asking that God minister to each member of this herd in a profound, special, and unique way.

I am praying for the healing you need, the restoration of your marriage, the new job, ministry calling, fun adventures, new careers, kids, education, friends' salvation, parking spots, and everything else I can imagine in prayer. But if there is one thing that I am asking God for in prayer it is that through praying for your elephants you come to know the God who loves you so much.

Before I finish, I need to share a story with you. During the writing of this book, God brought home one of the biggest elephant prayers of my life. That prayer was to one day become a lead pastor. It is something I have prayed about for over twenty-five years. It is an old elephant by spiritual elephant standards and one I thought might never show up.

Three days before I turned this book in to my editor as a finished work, I received the call that I had been confirmed as the new senior pastor of an amazing almost century-old church here in San Diego called La Jolla Christian Fellowship. If you are ever in town, please come visit so we can talk about your elephants. While I don't have time to tell you all the incredible things about this new adventure, there is one thing I must share that is extremely relevant to this book. The job comes with free rent.

Welcome to the herd, and keep believing and praying for your elephants!

NOTES

CHAPTER 1: PRAYING FOR YOUR ELEPHANT

1. Martin H. Manser, comp., *The Westminster Collection of Christian Quotations: Over 6,000 Quotations Arranged by Theme* (Louisville, KY: Westminster John Knox, 2001), 294.
2. E. M. Bounds, *The Weapon of Prayer* (Chicago: Moody, 1980), 9.
3. If you want to join the Praying for Your Elephant community, go to prayingforyourelephant.com.

CHAPTER 2: I DARE YOU

1. *Blue Letter Bible*, s.v. "thelō," www.blueletterbible.org/lang/lexicon/lexicon.cfm?Strongs=G2309.
2. "John 15:7," Bible Hub, http://biblehub.com/john/15-7.htm.
3. "John 15:7," Bible Hub, http://biblehub.com/john/15-7.htm.

CHAPTER 3: IDENTIFYING YOUR ELEPHANTS

1. Lewis Howes, "20 Lessons from Walt Disney on Entrepreneurship, Innovation and Chasing Your Dreams," *Forbes*, July 17, 2012, www.forbes.com/sites/lewishowes/2012/07/17/20-business-quotes-and-lessons-from-walt-disney/3/.

2. Gary Wolf, "Steve Jobs: The Next Insanely Great Thing," *Wired*, April 2, 1996, http://archive.wired.com/wired/archive/4.02/jobs_pr.html.

CHAPTER 4: LOST IN SPACE

1. "A Missiologist's Legacy: The Influence of Dr. Paul R. Orajala (Winter, 2006)," Nazarene Theological Seminary, http://nts.publishpath.com/a -missiologists-legacy-the-influence-of-dr-paul-r-orajala-winter-2006.
2. *Urban Dictionary*, s.v. "lost in translation," www.urbandictionary.com/define .php?term=lost+in+translation.
3. "Romans 8," Scripture 4 All, Greek/Hebrew interlinear Bible software, www.scripture4all.org/OnlineInterlinear/NTpdf/rom8.pdf.

CHAPTER 5: DIGGING FOR GOLD

1. C. S. Lewis, *The Screwtape Letters*, annotated ed. (New York: HarperOne, 2013), 22.

CHAPTER 8: EXTRA-VIRGIN

1. Sally Errico, "Olive Oil's Dark Side," *New Yorker*, February 8, 2012, www.newyorker.com/online/blogs/books/2012/02/the-exchange-tom -mueller.html.

CHAPTER 9: BE THE ANSWER

1. *Wikipedia*, s.v. "superstition," http://en.wikipedia.org/wiki/Superstition.
2. See the KJV and HCSB translations of Hebrews 11:1.
3. "The Efficacy of Prayer," *The Essential C. S. Lewis*, ed. Lyle W. Dorsett (New York: Touchstone, 1996), 378–79, 381.

CHAPTER 10: ELEPHANT WORSHIP

1. *Encyclopedia Britannica*, "Slavery," www.britannica.com/blackhistory /article-24157.

2. Alastair Jamieson, "Susan Boyle Could Be in Priory Clinic for Weeks, Says Doctor," *Telegraph*, June 3, 2009, www.telegraph.co.uk/culture /tvandradio/susan-boyle/5434811/Susan-Boyle-could-be-in-Priory-clinic-for-weeks-says-doctor.html.

CHAPTER 11: THE ELEPHANT GRAVEYARD

1. *Lincoln Observed: Civil War Dispatches of Noah Brooks*, ed. Michael Burlingame (Baltimore: Johns Hopkins University Press, 1998), 210.

BIBLE CREDITS

SMALL-GROUP DISCUSSION GUIDE

Praying for Your Elephant will be even more effective if read together within a prayer community. This discussion guide is a simple resource to help you do just that. Here, you will find questions that will spur dynamic discussion and encourage you to spend time together praying over the things that matter most to you. My hope is that as you prayerfully make your way through the book and begin praying game-changing prayers, God will begin to respond and encourage your community through answered prayer! **Each week after going through the discussion questions, I suggest you share how God has responded to some items on your elephant prayer list. Close your gathering by praying over one another's requests.**

CHAPTER 1
PRAYING FOR YOUR ELEPHANT

1. In this chapter I wrote about my struggle to pray for seemingly insignificant things. After further study, I discovered I was limiting my prayers and their potential. How do you feel you have limited the power of your prayers? Discuss.

2. This chapter challenges you to survey your prayer life. Share the results of that survey with the group. Where is your prayer life going strong, and where is it in need of attention?

3. This chapter proposes that asking prayer is not just about us but has a three-fold mission. How do you respond to that idea? In practical terms, how would your prayer life change if you embraced this new understanding of prayerful petition?

4. As I explained, many believers lack an understanding of what they are praying for. Is this true for you? Why or why not?

5. How could creating and tracking a list of one hundred strategic and specific prayer requests change your prayer life?

CHAPTER 2
I DARE YOU

1. Do you agree that it is a risky proposition to pray for anything in Jesus's name? Why or why not? What could be the potential challenges or blessings?

2. How can praying for anything in Jesus's name become reckless? Is it possible to go too far?

3. How has guilt impeded your prayer life? Have you felt too guilty to pray for certain requests?

4. I wrote about how I once prayed for a man's motorcycle to start. Have you ever stepped out in faith to pray for someone in public? What was the result?

5. Are there things you are too fearful to pray for? Discuss why that might be.

CHAPTER 3
IDENTIFYING YOUR ELEPHANTS

1. In this chapter I wrote about free-running our prayer lives, or having no structure or discipline in the manner in which we pray. How important is it to have a defined and structured prayer time?

2. How can we protect ourselves from legalism in our prayer life?

3. God's responses to our prayers often go far beyond what we originally asked. The book you are reading is one example of how God took a small, foolish prayer and magnified it into a much deeper purpose in my life. Share about a time when God answered one of your prayers in a manner above and beyond what you could have hoped for.

4. In this chapter I compared prayer to a salvage mission for sunken treasure. Do you agree that there are some purposes in our lives that will never be brought to the surface without prayer? Or will God have His way regardless of our prayers? Discuss.

5. I talked at length about the importance of spiritual imagination. Discuss the ways in which spending more time imagining more deeply into your prayers could change your prayer life.

CHAPTER 4
LOST IN SPACE

1. Have you ever been discouraged by your lack of expertise in prayer?

2. How have you addressed the problem of distractions during your prayer time? How do you stay focused in prayer?

3. Romans 8:26 states that no one knows how to pray. Do you find that a comfort or a discouragement?

4. The book of Romans mentions that the Holy Spirit helps us in our prayerful weakness. How have you experienced being helped in prayer by the Holy Spirit?

5. Experience is more important than expertise when it comes to prayer. Describe a powerful experience you have had in prayer.

CHAPTER 5
DIGGING FOR GOLD

1. In this chapter I discussed the challenge of keeping our prayer times consistent. How have you been able to stay consistent in prayer?

2. Do you ever find prayer boring or monotonous? How do you address this problem?

3. What do you do when you find yourself stuck in a prayer rut?

4. I spoke about the importance of staking a claim in the real estate of your personal time. Where do you have opportunities in your daily life to create some sacred and prayerful space?

5. Other than God's Word, the primary place you should be receiving direction from God is in prayer. Is this true for you, or do you depend more on other outside sources to find direction for life?

CHAPTER 6
OOMPA-LOOMPAS

1. Describe the balance of your current prayer life. Do you spend more time praying for others or for things related to yourself?

2. In this chapter I raise the issue of being disappointed when God does not answer our requests. This is especially true when we feel that we have done all the things He requires of us. Share about a time when you were disappointed with God's lack of response to your prayers.

3. How important is faith in seeing prayer answered?

4. One of the main purposes of prayer is to partner with God in the adventure of life. Have you ever seen prayer as an adventure? Describe one of your adventures with God in prayer.

5. Prayer can be a great form of evangelism. Have you ever employed prayer as an evangelism strategy? If so, what were the results? If not, discuss how you might employ prayer in this way.

CHAPTER 7
YOU CAN DO NOTHING

1. In this chapter I discuss the idea that when we do things in our own power, we lose the ability to have our actions remembered in eternity. What do you think about that concept?

2. What are some practical ways we can dedicate the things we do to God?

3. I write in this chapter about abiding prayer. What does it mean to abide in God? How could you more effectively abide in Him?

4. I wrote that prayer transfers the sap of God's will, intention, and power to the fruit of our lives and ministry. Describe some ways that God empowers you personally.

5. You are now more than halfway through the book. What changes are you already sensing in your prayer life?

CHAPTER 8
EXTRA-VIRGIN

1. This chapter highlights personal purity and holiness as a key to answered prayer. How do you feel holiness effects prayer?

2. What are some ways that sin hinders prayer?

3. As I mentioned in this chapter, many people just stop praying when they are caught up in sin. What are some better options or solutions?

4. What are some practical ways that we can consecrate ourselves before God?

5. God responded immediately to Daniel's humble and consecrated prayers. Share about a time when you experienced an immediate response to your prayers.

CHAPTER 9
BE THE ANSWER

1. In this chapter I wrote that the more we pray, the more we will actually be living in reality. How does prayer make your life more real?

2. This chapter focuses not only on praying but also on being the answer to others' prayer through kindness or acts of service. What are some tangible ways you could do this in your life?

3. William Temple is quoted as saying, "When I pray, coincidences happen, and when I don't pray, they don't." Share about a time when you found this to be true.

4. Oftentimes we must not only pray but also be willing to act. What are some things you can do to aid your prayers in becoming reality?

5. When has God used another believer's actions to answer a prayer request of yours?

CHAPTER 10
ELEPHANT WORSHIP

1. What are the three biggest elephants you are currently praying for? How long have you been praying for them?

2. How has praying for one of these very important requests shaped your walk with Christ?

3. In this chapter I wrote about elephant worship, which is the point when a prayer request becomes too important to us. How do we recognize when this has happened? How should we address it?

4. How would your relationship with Christ be affected if God never granted your most important request?

5. How has waiting for God to answer your request affected your contentment in Him?

CHAPTER 11
THE ELEPHANT GRAVEYARD

1. I write that praying for anything that matters deeply to us puts us at great risk. Why is this true?

2. This chapter highlights the story of Joseph. In the end, God fulfilled Joseph's dreams but perhaps not in the way he wanted. How would you respond if God chose not to answer your request in the way you expect?

3. I shared about the day when one of my elephant dreams died. Have you ever had a dream or desire—one you prayed about often—die? How did you handle it?

4. Have you ever been angry with God for not answering a request?

5. How can we live after the death of one of our sacred elephants?

CHAPTER 12
LAND GRAB

1. This chapter encourages us again to ask for anything in Jesus's name. What is one more massive elephant you could add to your list?

2. The story of the demon-possessed boy shows that God answered the prayers of a father who was lacking faith. Where are you lacking faith right now when it comes to praying for your elephants?

3. Reflect on the prayer that Jabez prayed. In what area of your life do you want to see your territory expanded or pain taken away?

4. I write about how prayer takes us into eternity and allows heaven's power to touch our lives. Have you experienced the power of prayer while reading this book?

5. What was your most important takeaway from *Praying for Your Elephant*?